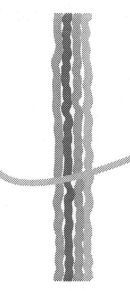

EXODUS

GATEWAY TO THE BIBLE

**MYRA B. NAGEL and
TRISH TOWLE GREEVES**

LEADER'S GUIDE

the KERYGMA
program

Art and Layout: Kathy Boykowycz

Exodus is published and distributed by The Kerygma Program, Suite 205, 300 Mt. Lebanon Boulevard, Pittsburgh, PA 15234.
Phone: 800/537-9462, FAX: 412/344-1823

ISBN 1-882236-43-2

The Kerygma Program
300 Mt. Lebanon Blvd.
Pittsburgh, PA 15234

CONTENTS

Introducing the Authors

MYRA B. NAGEL

Myra Nagel is an ordained minister in the United Church of Christ. A graduate of the University of Illinois and a member of Phi Beta Kappa, she received a Master of Divinity from Wesley Theological Seminary in Washington D.C. She has served churches in Vienna, Virginia and Port Charlotte, Florida, and has been an education consultant in the Potomac Association (Washington D.C. area) of the United Church of Christ.

Rev. Nagel is the author of two books, *Journey to the Cross* in 1966 and *Deliver Us from Evil: What the Bible Says about Satan*, just released. Both were published by the United Church Press. Recently she has retired from parish ministry in order to devote more time to writing and teaching. She and her husband Don live in Punta Gorda, Florida. She is a member of the Congregational United Church of Christ of Punta Gorda, where she teaches a weekly adult Bible study. She has written curricula for the ecumenical Discipleship Alive! Series and The Inviting Word, published by United Church Press.

TRISH TOWLE GREEVES

Trish Greeves is an ordained minister in the United Church of Christ, serving as Pastor of Union Congregational United Church of Christ in Elk River, Minnesota. She has previously served churches in Reston and Rock Spring, Virginia and in Minneapolis and Hutchinson, Minnesota. A native of Miami Beach, Florida and an honors graduate from Duke University, she was a computer systems analyst for the U.S. Navy Department and Sperry Univac and a self-employed consultant prior to receiving a Masters of Divinity from Virginia Theological Seminary in Alexandria, Virginia. She is the mother of two children.

Trish particularly enjoys teaching adult education classes that challenge participants to share their own faith as they explore the meaning and application of our Biblical heritage. Typical responses to her classes are: "I never knew Bible study could be such fun" and "I learned so much."

Myra Nagel and Trish Greeves are longtime friends.

Preparing to Lead a Kerygma Study Group

The Leader

This *Leader's Guide* has been developed to assist you in preparing to lead a group in a creative approach to the study of *Exodus: Gateway to the Bible*. Whether you are a clergy person, a church educator, or a lay person, it is less important how much you remember about your previous experiences in study groups than that you are now willing to engage in an intensive process of reading, studying, planning, and leading. There are no short cuts to successful leadership of a study group using the Kerygma approach. It will require a significant commitment of time and energy in order to design effective session plans for those who are engaged in this study with you.

As a leader of a Kerygma group, you will function in a variety of roles at different times. First of all, you will be a *learner*. Being a Kerygma leader will provide you with a wonderful opportunity to learn more about Exodus. You are not expected to be an expert on all of the material on which the course is based. However, you are expected to be prepared for each session so that you are able to guide the members of the group in a productive study.

As a result of your reading in preparation for leading each session, you will also become a *resource person*. You are not expected to know all the answers to every question that is raised, but you should be able to direct group members to resources that will assist them to find answers for themselves.

Furthermore, you will be a *planner* who works intentionally to consider session plan suggestions, the time available, the needs, interests, and abilities of the participants, and the resources needed to develop an appropriate plan for each session. The session plans provided in the *Leader's Guide* are very complete and probably offer more activities than you will be able to use in the time you have. However, the best session plans are ones you construct using the suggestions here as well as your own personal resources and experiences.

Being a *facilitator* of group process is also a very important role for you to perform. The fourteen session plans include many activities that involve participants in investigation, discussion, reflection, and application. The more comfortable you become in guiding these processes, the more effective the study will be for others. At first, some participants may prefer to have you tell them what they should know about the material. And, there will be times when you may be tempted to tell them all that you know. However, you will be most effective as a leader, and the group members will gain most from the course when they are guided by you in a variety of participatory activities as you explore the parables together.

Throughout the course of study you will also be called upon to exercise several important qualities. With the constraint of time and the great body of material to explore, you must be *flexible*. Unplanned questions will arise, activities will take longer than anticipated, and participants may want to go more slowly than you feel is necessary. In addition, you will need to be *patient* with the author when the written material seems to be confusing or unclear. And, unpredictable occurrences in the life of the group and in the life of the church will require patience.

Those Who Participate in Kerygma Groups

The people who choose to associate with a group that is studying the Bible using Kerygma resources do so for a variety of reasons and bring with them many levels of readiness and ability. When individuals are invited to attend a Kerygma group, they should be made aware from the beginning that this is not a study where the leader does all the work of preparation and presentation. Every participant is expected to have read the Basic Bible References and the appropriate material in the *Resource Book* prior to each session. Familiarity with this material is assumed by the session plans that are developed in the *Leader's Guide*.

Given the busy schedules of most people, there will be times when some come to a session with minimum preparation. You should not compromise the expectation of adequate preparation, because the experience for the whole group will suffer if the reading is not taken seriously. There are several ways you can handle the lack of preparation by participants.

1. Encourage persons who have not read the assignments to delay participation in the discussion until the others have had a chance.

2. Provide some time, as a part of your session plans, to review the key texts that serve as the foundation for the session.

3. When working in pairs or small groups, be sure that those who are not prepared are distributed among the groups rather than being placed together.

Some participants will have had a lot of experience with study groups, but for others this will be the first time they are involved in an in-depth study as adults. It is important for each person to feel that he or she belongs to the group. You will need to encourage both the experienced and inexperienced participants to be mindful and appreciative of each other.

Number of Sessions and Amount of Time

When planning to offer an adult course, it is important to ask and answer several key questions such as: How will this study fit into our adult education program? How many weeks or sessions will we schedule? How much time should be planned for each session? Perhaps these questions have already been answered in your church and the necessary arrangements have been made. If so, you and your group will have to adjust to what is already planned. If the questions have not been answered, you may want to consider a few options.

This *Leader's Guide* contains strategies for fourteen sessions. However, there are several ways to adjust the scheduling of those sessions: a) Fourteen sessions of one and a half to two hours each can be planned. The materials will work very well in this format. b) You can schedule your group to meet for one hour and expand the number of sessions to twenty-five or thirty. There is enough material to stretch the course over this period of time, but it will take some adapting on your part for each session to be complete with *Setting the Stage, Exploring the Scripture*, and *Closing*. c) If you are familiar with the material and have additional resources, you might use this course as the basis for designing your own program of study using several formats or modules.

The Printed Resources

A number of printed resources are included as part of *Exodus: The Gateway to the Bible*. Each resource makes a significant contribution to the whole program.

The Bible

The major curriculum resource for all Kerygma study programs is the Bible. The *New Revised Standard Version* is the translation on which this course is based. However, participants will be able to engage in the study effectively with another translation. In fact, the study will be enhanced by the presence of several translations. A study Bible with notes for each section of the text and other study aids is recommended for the leader as well as the participants. A number of such Bibles are available. Among those containing good study notes are the *New Oxford Annotated Bible with Apocrypha* (the *New Revised Standard Version* is the text for this Bible), *The Oxford Study Bible with Apocrypha*, and the *New Jerusalem Bible (with complete study notes)*.

The Resource Book

The *Resource Book* is the text both leaders and participants will use to guide their study. There are usually eight to ten pages of text in each chapter. This volume and the Bible contain all the necessary information to enable persons to participate profitably in the group sessions.

As you review the *Resource Book*, you will note that each chapter begins with a **Summary** and includes a list of **Basic Bible References** and a **Word List**. At the end of each chapter you will find a section entitled **For Further Study and Reflection**. You will want to review this section with the option of directing the group members' attention to it generally or on a week-by-week basis. From time to time this section will encourage participants to use additional study resources. For this purpose the group should have available from the church library several basic reference books, such as a Bible dictionary, commentaries and a dictionary of theological terms.

As a leader, you should read the *Resource Book* from beginning to end before you start planning any particular sessions. This effort will provide you with an overview of the total course. As you then plan for each session, you will need to reread the appropriate material.

The Leader's Guide

This is the book you have in your hands at this moment. It will be the indispensable resource you will use for planning each session. You will notice that each chapter of the *Leader's Guide* contains:

1. "Background from the Author." Dr. Gowan provides background information on the focus of the chapter and insights for leading your group.

2. "Session Plans." Extensive suggestions for session planning are provided for each chapter. Kerygma groups have been successfully led with the lecture and discussion format or with an emphasis on participatory activities. There is, however, overwhelming evidence that adult learning is increased and enhanced when group members participate directly in the learning process. It is strongly recommended that all leaders review the session plans and incorporate as many suggestions as appropriate into each session.

Planning the Group Sessions

The first group session will be most effective if you distribute copies of the *Resource Book* to members of the group ahead of time. Tell them to read the Introduction and Chapter One and to bring any questions that arise from the reading to the session.

By reading the *Resource Book*, the Bible texts, the *Leader's Guide*, and supplementary resources, you will have completed a major part of preparing to lead a study session. However, there is one more important task: preparing a workable session plan to use with *your* group. Even though a detailed outline of a plan is provided for each session, it is important to prepare *your own* session plan appropriate for *your* group. Only you know the unique situation of your group: the number of participants; the amount of time for each session; the interests, abilities, and needs of each participant; and circumstances of the ministry of your church. Thus, you are the only one who can prepare a session plan that is truly appropriate for your group.

In your plan you will want to give special attention to the following elements that appear at the beginning of each chapter of the *Resource Book*:

1. *Summary*. This is the focus of the chapter. All that you and the participants will do during the group session will be done to uncover the meaning of this brief summary statement.

2. *Basic Bible References*. These are the essential references that you and the participants must read. These Bible texts provide the basis for the group session. They will be used in one or another of the suggested activities.

3. *Word List*. These words or phrases are important terms included in the *Resource Book* or the biblical texts of the study. They may be unfamiliar to many members of your group. Yet they are words for which you, as the leader, should have working definitions.

The Session Plans in the Leader's Guide Include:

1. *Learning Objectives*. The three or four statements presenting learning objectives indicate what the leader will help the participants to accomplish as a result of their study. It is appropriate to share these objectives with the members of the group at the beginning of each session. The selection of activities is then guided by the objectives considered most important. The learning objectives can also be used as a basis for evaluating whether you and the participants have accomplished what was intended. A word of caution: accomplishing the learning objectives is not all there is to leading a study group. Some of the most important things that happen among the participants cannot be evaluated by learning objectives: things such as forming a Christian community, growing in faith, developing the ability to speak comfortably about one's faith, nurturing the spiritual life, and other important matters regarding the Christian faith.

2. *Resources You May Need*. In addition to the Bible and *Resource Book*, a list of those items needed for the various activities is provided.

3. *Leadership Strategy*. This is the heart of the session plan. The leadership strategy is organized in four sections:

   a. "Setting the Stage" is a time for inviting participants to become involved with the subject of the session. Ordinarily it will take ten to fifteen minutes for this segment of the session.

   b. "Exploring the Scripture" is what the study is all about. Most of the time of the session will be spent with activities that involve exploration of biblical texts which are integral to the theme. Usually two or three activities will be planned for this portion of the session.

c. "Closing" is a time to bring closure to the session, to summarize what has been explored, and to suggest applications of what has been learned to one's own faith and life experiences.

4. *Looking Ahead.* In order to work effectively at the next session, some or all of the participants may need to do some special preparation. For example, a brief report requiring some research is occasionally called for in the session plans. Participants are invited to volunteer for these assignments. Of course, the basic assignment for each week is reading the *Resource Book* and the recommended Bible texts.

5. *Worksheets.* These pages in the *Leader's Guide* may be duplicated for use in the session activities.

The basic supplemental resource for this study is Dr. Gowan's book *Theology in Exodus: Biblical Theology in the Form of a Commentary.* (Louisville: Westminster John Knox Press, 1994). This volume is available from the Kerygma office. To order use the address and telephone number on the title page of this *Guide*.

Using Leadership Strategies

As you read the suggestions in each Leadership Strategy, you will notice that several activities are usually offered for each segment of the session. These activities are clearly separated by **or, and**, or **and/or** in the center of the page. Ordinarily no group would be expected to complete all the activities that are included for each session. And there will be times when you, as the leader, will decide to do something different from what is suggested. You should feel free to utilize your own creativity, but be sure that what you do relates directly to the theme and learning objectives of the session.

When choosing from among the options that are suggested, there are several things to keep in mind:

1. The *amount of time* available is a critical factor which will influence your decision. When faced with the choice of trying to do two activities quickly (perhaps superficially) or doing one activity thoroughly, it is usually best to do the one activity.

2. *Activities that involve participants* interacting with one another, preparing a presentation to share with others, or working cooperatively on a task, will always take more time than it takes for the leader to present the same information. However, when group members are significantly involved in the process of their own learning, they will be much more motivated and will accomplish more in the end.

3. Some activities are designed to probe *in depth*, and others are intended to provide an *overview*. In addition, there are activities for individuals or pairs or small groups or the whole group. The important thing is to develop a session plan that has balance, so that there are some in-depth and some overview activities. There also needs to be a balance among individual, small-group, and whole-group activities.

4. The *interests, abilities*, and *previous experience* of the members of the group will influence your choices regarding which of the suggested activities to implement. It is important for you to become acquainted with the members of the group in order to make such judgments. It may be self-defeating to plan an activity that you feel will be resisted by many in the group.

5. Your own *interests, skills*, and *concerns* must also be considered when deciding which activities to choose. You should be reasonably comfortable with an activity and confident that it can be used effectively to guide the group's study. However, as the course develops and you become comfortable with the group and the subject matter, you should be willing to try some of the activities that are new to you.

Planning for leading a study group is an art. There is no right session plan for every topic or every situation or every leader. Neither is there just one right way to go about planning. Practice the art of planning until you find a process that works effectively for you.

A Final Word

You are about to embark on a wonderful journey with a number of companions. This time together has the potential for building relationships among those who participate, for increasing their knowledge and appreciation of the Book of Exodus, and for providing a time of spiritual nurture and renewal. May this be a period of fruitful study and reflection for you and those who join you on the journey.

Additional Leadership Resources

In addition to the preceding suggestions, Kerygma has available several resources which will assist you in developing your leadership skills:

Session Planning Form. This form provides a way for you to organize your plans for each session. It is found at the end of this section. Feel free to make as many copies as you need.

Guidelines for Adult Education. These guidelines summarize ten general principles on which contemporary effective adult education is based. They will be found on the following pages.

Adult Education Idea Book. This resource provides a comprehensive design for establishing an effective program of adult education. It includes chapters on "Leadership and Leadership Development" and "Fifty Great Ideas to Help Promote Adult Bible Study in Your Church". This book is available from the Kerygma office.

Guidelines for Adult Education

The following guidelines provide a summary of the convictions about adult education on which the Kerygma resources are based:

- **Adults are responsible for their own learning.**

  Therefore, it is important not to develop dependent relationships whereby the learners look to the leader as the authority and primary source of information.

- **Adults learn best when they can participate directly in the process of their own learning.**

  Therefore, opportunities should be provided in each session for participants to make decisions about what and how they will learn and to interact with the subject matter and other learners.

- **Adults represent a variety of learning styles as well as different stages of physical, emotional, and spiritual development.**

  Therefore, learners will be related to individually without assuming that all adults are the same. Learners will be encouraged to work at their own pace and to make applications that are appropriate to themselves.

- **Learning is reinforced best when adults have the opportunity to practice skills and to express ideas in their own words.**

  Therefore, in each session there will be opportunities to practice particular skills and to express personal insights and interpretation.

- **Learning occurs within an environment of trusting relationships.**

  Therefore, it is important to develop a process whereby persons will be encouraged to share feelings, needs, and concerns as well as information and ideas. In such a setting persons will be helped to become caring about and supportive of one another.

- **It is not necessary to use competitive activities to motivate adults to participate and learn.**

  Therefore, the activities and resources will represent a cooperative, collaborative style of learning.

- **Adults who have positive self-concepts are less threatened by new information and experiences.**

  Therefore, leaders will be encouraged to use strategies that enhance a person's sense of self-worth.

- **Adults will increase their knowledge and skill to a greater extent when they gain a sense of satisfaction and experience success in those activities that are planned for them.**

  Therefore, the session plans of the Kerygma Program study resources will present a variety of activities that are designed to enable participants to achieve satisfaction and success.

Session Planning Form

Course Name _____

Session _____

Learning Objectives:

Time	Strategies/Activities	Resources

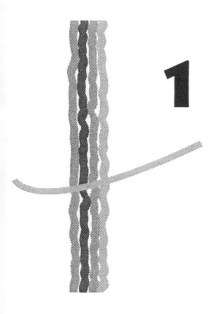

INTRODUCTION: THE BOOK OF EXODUS AND BIBLICAL THEOLOGY

1

Background from the Author

In this course we will provide an extended example of an essential principle of biblical interpretation: using the testimony of the *whole Bible* in order to learn what God intends to say to us, rather than focusing on single texts. Sometimes this is called letting Scripture interpret Scripture. It differs from the old proof-texting approach, which assumed that each text in the Bible somehow contains the "whole truth." That always involves selecting the texts that support what one wants to believe. Unfortunately, the result is then likely to be the mistaken conclusion that the Bible seems to contradict itself, for one proof-text can often be countered by another. God's revelation is to be found in the message of scripture as a whole, rather than in isolated texts.

When one looks for the whole biblical message on a given theme it will be seen that there is a consistency that prevails over apparent discrepancies. Within the long tradition recorded in Scripture there will be variations, certainly, for different circumstances led people to see things differently, and new problems or needs would lead to emphasis on different parts of the tradition. Something that had seemed important at an early time might be left behind as times changed. Every generation of believers, however, has continued to reaffirm and reapply what it has discovered to be the essentials of the faith, and it is the consistent tradition that we can trace through Scripture which should be understood as the word of God to us. We shall not be content, then, with the message of Exodus alone, but will use it as our starting point for tracing the message to us of the whole Bible.

You will notice that we do not begin with the text of the book of Exodus until the next session. In this session your work with Scripture will involve a survey of a series of passages that use materials from Exodus in various ways. There are two primary aims for the session: 1) To be clear about how the book of Exodus will be used as a way of working with key topics in theology. 2) To become aware of the importance of two subjects, exodus and Sinai, by noting the various ways the authors of Scripture used them.

This is not a course in the history of Israel. But when we study Exodus, historical questions are bound to arise, as a brief section in the first session has acknowledged. Since the course deals with Biblical Theology, discussions of history are kept to a minimum in the *Resource Book*, but questions of historicity cannot be completely ignored. Judaism and Christianity are historical religions, not simply proclamations of spiritual truths. That is, they are based on claims that certain events in human history were acts of God, who is revealed through them. The biblical writers claimed that truth about God can be learned from what God has done. So, if events that are claimed to be revelations of God did not happen, have we believed in vain? History cannot be ignored.

In this session some historical evidence for the time of the exodus has been offered, but it had to be admitted that not much data is available. This can lead some to skeptical conclusions, but this course is written from the point of view that the exodus did in fact occur, even though there remains much uncertainty about the details of the event. My understanding of it is stated briefly: I work back from the later existence of Israel, with its unique faith (about which we have abundant historical evidence), and conclude from this that the essentials of the Exodus story provide the most likely explanation for the appearance of that people, with that faith. Since details are uncertain, it seems best not to spend much time on them, and to focus instead on what is clear in Scripture: the faith of Israel that came into existence as a result of that event, and the way that faith has become gospel for us.

My book, *Theology in Exodus: Biblical Theology in the Form of a Commentary* (Louisville; Westminster John Knox Press, 1994), will provide a fairly complete guide to this way of studying Scripture for those topics introduced by Exodus that might be called the "doctrine of God." It is recommended that leaders regularly make use of the additional material in this volume. The fuller comments on Biblical Theology in the Introduction to the book (pages ix-xviii) should be helpful in preparing for this session. When topics other than the doctrine of God are introduced by Exodus (e.g. Passover), suggestions of additional resources will be made in these Background Notes.

Additional Resources:

A very complete commentary that will be useful at many points along the way is: Brevard S. Childs, *The Book of Exodus* (Old Testament Library; Philadelphia: Westminster Press, 1974). A shorter volume focused on the theology of the book, and thus likely to be helpful at many points is: Terence E. Fretheim, *Exodus* (Interpretation; Atlanta: John Knox Press, 1991). Participants will be asked to use a concordance of the Bible at times, and will be referred to a Bible dictionary for more complete articles on certain topics. A map of the Sinai peninsula will be helpful in connection with Sessions 7 and 8.

SESSION PLANS

Learning Objectives

This session is intended to enable participants to:

1. Get to know one another.

2. Define biblical theology in their own words.

3. Name several ways Exodus themes are reflected in later scripture.

4. Place the Exodus in the context of other major events in Israel's early life.

Resources You May Need

Plastic name tags or yarn and posterboard or construction paper

3 x 5 cards or slips of paper, string and clothespins

Chalkboard or newsprint and markers

Bibles and copies of the worksheet "Exodus Themes in Later Scripture"

Copies of "Exodus Themes in Later Scripture"

Copies of "Litany on Psalm 136"

Copies of "A Reading From Hebrews"

Leadership Strategy

SETTING THE STAGE

1. **Name tags.** Provide name tags that can be worn for the next several sessions. Use the clip-on variety with plastic covers or make necklace-style name tags using colored yarn and "medallions" cut from light posterboard, card stock, or construction paper. (5-10 minutes)

2. **Welcome.** Welcome the group. Attend to any necessary "housekeeping" details such as announcing the meeting dates and the location of restroom facilities, providing sign-up sheets for refreshments, collecting registration fees, and distributing *Resource Books*. (5 minutes)

    Explain that it is hoped that members of the group will make new friends, but that they may sit with whomever they wish. One good arrangement for this type of study is to have people gathered around tables in groups of five or six. This provides a surface for books and papers, and participants are already in natural groups for discussion. Angle the tables so that everyone can see the leader, newsprint and/or chalkboard.

    It is important that everyone knows that the sessions will begin and end on time. If you consistently wait for latecomers, or are late yourself, participants will come later and later, knowing that things take a while to get going. To keep to your posted ending hour honors the time commitment participants have made for this study.

3. If the *Resource Books* were not distributed prior to this first session, do that now. Invite participants to turn to the Table of Contents. Tell them it is expected that before each session they will have read the appropriate chapter in the *Resource Book* and the Basic Bible references. Encourage them to note any questions that arise from this reading, so they can be brought to the group sessions for discussion.

(In the session plans which follow we have not included a section for dealing with questions participants bring to the group from their preparation. Some leaders designate time to consider these issues in each session. Others deal with questions as they arise or when they are related to other topics being discussed.)

Then ask everyone to turn to the section entitled "Preparing for the Group Sessions." Summarize this material, pointing out the various components of each chapter. Add comments from your own experience in preparing for this course and others like it.

4. **Opening Prayer**. Pray in your own words or read the following prayer:

Gracious God, you led your people out of Egypt into the land of your promise, and you have led each one of us from the busyness of our lives into a new journey of promise and faith. Grant us courage to risk entering unexplored places within our lives; guide us safely through any wilderness we may encounter; light our footsteps with the lamp of your Word; teach us the joy of your companionship; and lead us ever closer to your heart. In the name of Christ, our companion and guide, we pray. Amen. (2 minutes)

5. **Sharing Memories**. Divide the participants into groups of 3-4 and invite them to tell each other about an experience or event that caused them to see themselves in a new way and to tell how that new perception has influenced their lives. Some examples are cutting childhood braids, mastering a difficult skill, being chosen or elected to a position, growing a beard, receiving a first kiss, having a baby, losing a parent. Before dividing into groups, introduce the activity by telling a personal example. After about 15 minutes of storytelling in small groups, bring the whole group together. Conclude the activity by observing that the Exodus event dramatically changed the way the people of Israel saw themselves. From that point on, they saw themselves as God's people—chosen, blessed, and called. As we study Exodus, we will consider how that new perception influenced the whole biblical story and continues to shape our lives today. (20 minutes)

or

Stories about Ancestors. In groups of 3-4, invite the participants to tell something one of their ancestors (grandparent, great grandparent) did that has had a continuing influence on them and their family. What beliefs, values, or directions has this encouraged or discouraged? How has the story changed as it has been retold? After 15 minutes, bring the group back together. Conclude the activity by saying that just as stories from our family's past continue to influence us, the story of the Exodus event continues to interpret and shape our faith even today. (20 minutes).

or

Self-Introductions. Invite the group members to introduce themselves and share a few words about why they are participating in this study. If the group is larger than 10, divide into groups of 6-8 for the introductions. (10-20 minutes)

EXPLORING THE SCRIPTURE

1. **Biblical Theology.** Briefly introduce the concept of Biblical Theology, summarizing ideas from the *Resource Book* (pages 3-5), including the following points:

   • *Theology* is one's carefully thought-through statement about what one believes about God and one's relationship to God.

   • *Biblical Theology* follows the biblical narrative, discerning what God is like by watching what God does.

   • *Exodus* is a good starting point for doing "biblical theology" because the themes that occur in Exodus also appear elsewhere.

   • Theology is the *work of all Christians*, not merely repeating others' thoughts, but making our own confessions. (3-5 minutes)

2. **Exodus as a Starting Point for Theology.** Observe that Exodus is a good place to begin a study of biblical theology because many of its insights about God form themes that are foundational for the whole Bible.

   On chalkboard or newsprint, list the following Exodus themes, drawing on information in the section, "The Value of Exodus as a Starting Point" in the *Resource Book*:

   • **God as Deliverer** (from oppression in Egypt)

   • **Covenant and Law** (given at Mt. Sinai)

- **God's nature** (revealed in God's name)

- **Community** (God's people)

- **Human Sin and God's Forgiveness** (the Golden Calf incident).

About each theme ask, "Where else in the Bible do these themes occur?" Write the participants' responses for each theme in short phrases on the chalkboard or newsprint. Participants may require some assistance at this point. Suggest that they open their *Resource Books* to pages 5-6 to discover the relevant passages in Exodus and use their study Bibles to discover other passages. Encourage them also to draw on their general knowledge of the Bible. Conclude by noting that throughout the study of Exodus we will continue to see how Exodus themes are reflected in Scripture. (10 minutes)

or

Exodus Themes in Later Scripture. Distribute the worksheet "Exodus Themes in Later Scripture." Divide into groups of 3-6. Number the groups and assign each group the passage from the worksheet that corresponds to its group number. Smaller groups need not use all the passages. Ask the groups to read their passages, discuss them briefly, and fill out the worksheet. Suggest that each group appoint a spokesperson to share its worksheet.

While the groups are meeting, list on chalkboard or newsprint the 5 Exodus themes from the worksheet: God as Deliverer, Covenant and Law, God's Nature, Community, and Human Sin and Forgiveness. Leave space after each theme. After about 15 minutes, bring the whole group together and have each group report on its discussion. As each group reports, write its ideas under the appropriate theme. Conclude by noting that throughout the study we will continue to observe how the insights about God in Exodus are foundational for later Old Testament and New Testament thought. (30 minutes)

3. **Describing God.** Ask, "Remembering what we have observed about God's actions, what are some words you would use to describe the God of the Bible?" Participants may suggest words like "deliverer," "compassionate," "strong," or

"caring." List their suggestions on chalkboard or newsprint. Note that in the process of gaining insights about God and observing how these insights are reflected throughout Scripture, we have begun to formulate biblical theology. This process will continue throughout the study. (5 minutes)

or

Describing God's Actions. Distribute the "Litany on Psalm 136." Have participants read it silently and complete the sentence on the litany, "For me, O God, you are the One who . . ." As in the exercise above, note that this process of formulating biblical theology will continue throughout the study. (8 minutes)

4. **Living Time Line.** In this introductory session, the group will benefit from setting Exodus into its historical context. Ahead of time, print each of the following events on separate 3 x 5 cards. Give one to each person in the group. Add or eliminate events as necessary to provide one for each person. Have the participants form a "living time line," arranging themselves so the events are in order. Review the order of events, rearranging group members as needed. Groups with fewer than 10 members might work together to lay the cards in order on a table or to clip them with clothespins to a string you have stretched clothesline-fashion from two points in the room.

   a. Creation

   b. Call of Abraham

   c. Birth of Jacob's 12 sons (founders of Israel's 12 tribes)

   d. Joseph traded into slavery

   e. Captivity in Egypt

   f. Call of Moses

   g. 10 Plagues

   h. Deliverance at the Red Sea

   i. Covenant at Sinai

   j. Joshua leads people of Israel into Canaan

k. Samuel anoints Saul King of Israel

l. David becomes King of Israel

m. Northern tribes secede to divide the Kingdom of Israel

n. Hosea's life and preaching to Northern Kingdom

o. Babylonian captivity

p. Building of the Second Temple

q. Herod the Great becomes king

r. Birth of Jesus

s. Feeding of the 5000

t. The Last Supper

u. Paul's missionary journeys (20 minutes)

or

Historical Overview. Draw the following time line on the board and give a brief overview of Biblical history to set Exodus within the time frame of the major historical events up to the birth of Jesus. Review Dr. Gowan's comments on Exodus history in the "Background from the Author" material. Dates are taken from Bernhard W. Anderson, *Understanding the Old Testament*: Abridged Fourth Edition (New Jersey: Prentice Hall, 1998).

	BCE
Call of Abraham	(c.1800)
Exodus	(c. 1290-1250)
Entry into Canaan	(c. 1250-1200)
Monarchy established	(c. 1020)
Fall of Northern Kingdom to Assyria	(722)
Fall of Judah/Exile in Babylon	(587)
Return/Rebuilding Temple	(520-515)
Jesus' life, death, and resurrection	(6-4 BCE to 30-33 CE)

Paul's journeys   (47-49 CE to 56)

New Testament written   (1,2 Thessalonians, CE 50-52)

                                                        (Mark CE 68-70; 2 Peter 130-150)

(10 minutes)

and

Historical Basis for Exodus. In addition to setting Exodus in its context within the biblical story, group members will want to know how it fits into the history of ancient Egypt. Summarize briefly Dr. Gowan's answers to the question, "But What Really Happened in Egypt and Sinai?" from the *Resource Book*. Note especially the probable date around 1250 BCE and the author's opinion that although scholars have little evidence for the Exodus event outside the Bible, "the Israel of later times would never have come into existence unless something very much like this had happened." (5 minutes)

CLOSING

A Litany. Read the "Litany on Psalm 136" with everyone reading the responses printed in bold. If the group has completed the sentence, "For me, O God, you are the one who . . .," invite all who wish to do so to speak their completed sentences. After each person's sentence, the group may repeat the response, "for your steadfast love endures forever." (5 minutes)

or

A Reading from Hebrews. Read aloud "A Reading from Hebrews." Select volunteers to read the first 6 sections. All join in the last section, printed in bold. (5 minutes)

and/or

Prayer. Pray in your own words, incorporating into the prayer some thoughts the group has expressed. Your prayer might begin, "O God, you are . . . (words from their list describing God) or "O God, you are the one who . . . (some of God's actions from their list). Close by asking God to guide and bless the group as they journey together through Exodus. (3 minutes)

Looking Ahead

One of the options in the next session involves studying hymns. You will need to locate appropriate hymns for this activity ahead of time. Your church hymnal may contain many of the hymns suggested. Your minister and your church library may also have some hymnals where other hymns may be found.

If you plan to close with the hymn, "O God, My God," (*New Century Hymnal* #515), make copies of this hymn. You might ask a good vocalist in your congregation to make a tape recording of this hymn for you to use.

Session 6 suggests inviting a Jewish rabbi to talk to the group and/or to lead a Seder meal. If you choose this option, you will want to invite the rabbi well in advance and to follow a verbal invitation with a letter confirming the date, outlining your expectations, and asking what materials you need to prepare.

Exodus Themes in Later Scripture

Read the Bible passage below that corresponds to your group number and follow the instructions below:

1. Joshua 24:1-8,14-15

2. Deuteronomy 26:1-11

3. Psalm 105:23-42

4. Psalm 106:6-16,47-48

5. Acts 7:17-41

6. Hebrews 11:23-29

Which of the following themes introduced in Exodus are reflected in your passage? Working together as a group, write a summary under the appropriate heading(s). Appoint a spokesperson to make a brief report on your discussion to the whole group.

- **God as Deliverer**

- **Covenant and Law**

- **God's Nature**

- **Community**

- **Human Sin and God's Forgiveness**

Litany on Psalm 136

O God, you brought Israel out from among the Egyptians, with a strong hand and an outstretched arm.

for your steadfast love endures forever.

You divided the Red Sea in two, and made Israel pass through the midst of it,

for your steadfast love endures forever.

You led your people through the wilderness,

for your steadfast love endures forever.

You remember us in our low estate; you rescue us from our distress;

you give food to all flesh,

for your steadfast love endures forever.

For me, O God, you are the one who _____

_____ ,

for your steadfast love endures forever.

We give thanks to you, O God of heaven,

for your steadfast love endures forever.

. . . based on Psalm 136:10-16,23-26

A Reading from Hebrews

1) Now faith is the assurance of things hoped for, the conviction of things not seen. Indeed, by faith our ancestors received approval.

2) By faith, Moses was hidden by his parents for three months after his birth, because they saw that the child was beautiful, and they were not afraid of the king's edict.

3) By faith, Moses, when he was grown up, refused to be called a son of Pharaoh's daughter, choosing rather to share ill-treatment with the people of God than to enjoy the fleeting pleasures of sin. . . .

4) By faith, he left Egypt, unafraid of the king's anger; for he persevered as though he saw him who is invisible.

5) By faith, he kept the Passover and the sprinkling of blood, so that the destroyer of the firstborn would not touch the firstborn of Israel.

6) By faith, the people passed through the Red Sea as if it were dry land, but when the Egyptians attempted to do so they were drowned. . . .

All: Therefore, since we are surrounded by so great a cloud of witnesses, let us also lay aside every weight and the sin that clings so closely, and let us run with perseverance the race that is set before us, looking to Jesus the pioneer and prefecture of our faith, who for the sake of the joy that was set before him endured the cross, disregarding its shame, and has taken his seat at the right hand of the throne of God.

. . . Hebrews 11:1-2,23-29;12:1-2

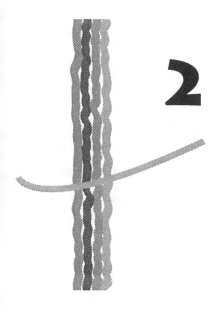

2

DARKNESS: LIFE AND DEATH IN EGYPT

Background from the Author

You may anticipate three different reactions to the way I have read Exodus 1-2:

1. Some will question whether I have been correct in saying that the author has written these chapters as if God was absent from the lives of the Hebrews during this period. The familiar way of reading them is to claim that God was always active, but behind the scenes. My response is that we may well believe that (as I do), and the author may have believed that, but that is not how he told the story. In my book, I suggest the way he might have told it (p. 3), with God present all along the way. Since he did not, it seems to me that the author deliberately wanted to speak of a time when God *seemed* to be inactive.

2. The second reaction will be, "Are you saying God was really absent and doing nothing?" That is why I emphasized *seemed*. We do not know what is going on in heaven, and as mentioned above, I believe God is always present and always active. The point of this session is, however, that there are times in life when people see no evidence of that. For all we know, based on what we can see, God is not doing anything. That is real life for some of us, and it produces the terrible tensions between faith and experience that are expressed so fervently in the Psalms of Lament. So, our subject is not what God is *really* doing, but the way we *feel* when life doesn't seem to make sense.

3. For some, the above questions will not occur, because this subject matter speaks very directly to them. They have felt (or maybe do feel) exactly the way the Psalmists felt when they prayed the laments, so this session may be very important for them.

The boldness, even fierceness, of the language of the Psalms of Lament sometimes troubles Christians. The reaction may be to say this is Old Testament language; Christians shouldn't pray this way. If this subject comes up, a quote from Calvin's commentary on the Psalms may provide a helpful starting point. (Not without reason, it is my custom to call this book *An Anatomy of All the Parts of the Soul*.)

> Since there is no emotion anyone will experience
>
> Whose image is not reflected in this mirror.
>
> Indeed, here the Holy Spirit has drawn to the life
>
> All pains, sorrows, fears, doubts,
>
> Hates, cares, anxieties—
>
> In short—all the turbulent emotions
>
> With which men's minds are commonly stirred.
>
> The rest of the Scriptures contains
>
> The commandments that God enjoined upon His servants
>
> To announce to us.
>
> But here the prophets themselves
>
> Speaking with God
>
> Uncover all their inner feelings
>
> And call, or rather drag,
>
> Each one of us to examine himself.[1]

Our full humanity is reflected in the Psalms, including the emotions we ought to control, such as doubt and hate and the desire for revenge. Nevertheless they will appear at times, whether we like it or not. If we can't avoid them, what do we do with them? The Psalms say, take them to God and leave them with God. The Psalms teach us that we *may* pray this way, and that can be a liberating discovery for some Christians. "It's all right to yell at God," and God will listen, and answer.

---

[1] Translation taken from *The Piety of John Calvin: An Anthology Illustrative of the Spirituality of the Reformer*, translated and edited by Ford Lewis Battles (Grand Rapids: Baker Book House, 1978) pp. 27-28.

I have offered an understanding of Jesus' "cry of dereliction" from the cross that takes it literally and very seriously. If it can be accepted, it leads us into the mystery of God taking upon himself the very depths of human distress. It requires us to believe in the full humanity and the full divinity of Christ, as the creeds of the church teach it. For some, the fact that this defies human logic will be a problem. If that comes up, you may need to consult a resource explaining why Christianity has insisted that this must be true, for Christ to be our savior, even though we cannot fully understand it. A classic statement is St. Anselm's *Why God Became Man*. D. M. Baillie wrote an excellent contemporary study: *God Was In Christ* (New York: Charles Scribner's Sons, 1948).

SESSION PLANS

Learning Objectives

This session is intended to enable participants to:

1. Summarize the story told in Exodus 1-2.

2. Compare some of their own experiences of struggle and hardship to the Israelites' situation in Egypt.

3. Apply biblical examples of lament, remembering, and waiting to their own faith life.

4. Describe how the story of Jesus can make them feel closer to God.

Resources You May Need

Chalkboard or newsprint and markers

3 x 5 cards or slips of paper

Drawing paper (8-1/2 x 11) and crayons or markers

A variety of hymnals

Copies of Worksheet A "Psalm 22," Worksheet B "Cries for Help in Hymns," and the "Litany of Lament"

Leadership Strategy

SETTING THE STAGE

1. **Welcome.** Welcome everyone back. If there are people attending for the first time, invite all group members to introduce themselves. Continue to encourage use of the name tags. (5 minutes)

2. **Prayer from the Psalms.** Read Psalm 61:1-3. You will find this reading in the Appendix, "Prayers from the Psalms," which contains an opening Psalm-prayer for each session. If you plan to open most sessions by having the group read a Psalm together, you may wish to copy the whole Psalm resource and distribute it at this session. The Psalm-prayers may be read responsively. (3 minutes)

and/or

Opening Prayer. Offer a prayer asking for God's presence with the group. (3 minutes)

3. **Personal Stories.** Remind the group that Exodus begins at a dark moment when people did not know God as an active participant in their lives. Today's session invites us to talk about times when we too may have found ourselves unable to sense God's presence in our lives.

Invite participants to think about a time of despair, hopelessness, struggle, loss, hurt, etc., when they have felt forgotten by God or unable to sense God's care or presence. Have each person draw a picture or symbol that represents his feelings at that time. After 10-15 minutes, divide into groups of 3-4 to share their experiences and pictures (to whatever extent they are comfortable doing so). What was happening? What helped them through it? What, if anything, did they learn? How did it affect their relationship to God? Conclude by saying that remembering dark moments in our own lives can help us relate to the Israelites' situation in Egypt. (20 minutes)

or

Listing Times of Darkness. As in the exercise above, remind the group that Exodus begins at a dark moment when people did not know God as an active participant in their lives. Invite the group to suggest times of darkness from their own lives or in the life of the world, times when it may have been difficult to see evidence of God's activity. Their suggestions may include death of a child, loss of a job, flood or hurricane, the Holocaust, ethnic cleansing in the former Yugoslavia, killing of innocents in drug wars. List their suggestions on chalkboard or newsprint. Conclude by saying that listing contemporary situations of darkness helps us get in touch with the feelings of the Hebrew slaves in Egypt as the story of Exodus begins. (10 minutes)

EXPLORING THE SCRIPTURE

1. **Naming the Cast.** Invite the group to call out the names of the major participants of the story mentioned between 1:8 and 2:23 and list them on chalkboard or newsprint. Ask "What were his or her circumstances? How did he or she respond to those circumstances?" in relation to each character. List responses with each name. (10 minutes)

or

Writing Monologues. Write the following names on 3 x 5 cards or slips of paper:

1. A midwife (Shiphrah or Puah)

2. Moses' sister (Miriam)

3. Moses' mother (Jochebed)

4. Pharaoh's Daughter

5. Moses

Divide into 5 small groups, giving one name to each group. Ask the groups to imagine how their assigned persons saw their own circumstances. What were their options? How would they describe and explain what they did? Have each group pretend to be the person named on the card and write a brief monologue representing that person's "testimony" using the first person "I." (For example, "I am Shiphrah, and I have a story to tell you.") After about 10 minutes, bring the large group together and invite a spokesperson for each group to present the character's "testimony." (20 minutes)

2. **Introducing the Theme of Lament.** Observe that Exodus 1-2, up until 2:23, is written as *if* God were absent. The people seem to be left on their own. This does not mean God *actually* was absent, but rather that God *seemed* absent. In Exodus 2:23-25, God enters the picture!

Ask a volunteer to read 2:23-25 aloud. Then, drawing information from the section "When God Seems to Do Nothing" in the *Resource Book*, explain that the author of Exodus probably used the verbs God *heard*, God *remembered*, God *saw*, and God *knew* because these verbs occurred frequently in Psalms of Lament. (5 minutes)

and

Listing Lament Language. Give each member of the group a 3 x 5 card or slip of paper on which you have written one of the scripture passages below. You may need to give some of the passages to more than one person or divide into small groups and give a passage to each group.

Psalm 10:1-2	Psalm 10:3-4	Psalm 35:17,22-23
Psalm 44:17-26	Psalm 89:46-51	Isaiah 64:7-12
Job 24:9-12	Psalm 22:1-2,11,19	

After the group members have looked up their passages, invite them to call out questions, complaints or phrases that express the writer's perception of God's absence. List these phrases on chalkboard or newsprint, compiling a collage of lament language. Ask, "How do these words make you feel?" After a few minutes, talk to the group about the lament as a form of prayer, reminding them that there is no thought, feeling, or experience we cannot express to God. (15-20 minutes)

and/or

Writing a Lament. After reading Exodus 2:23-25 aloud as described above, ask, "What are some words the Hebrews might have said as they *groaned* and *cried out*?" Suggest phrases like "Help me!" "Where are you?" "Don't forget me!" "Save me!" List other suggestions on chalkboard or newsprint.

Invite each group member to write a lament based upon a personal experience or social situation that causes grief or struggle. Suggest that participants include in their laments some of the words from the list they have just made. To help them get started, write the following outline on chalkboard or newsprint.

When I think about . . . (situation)

I . . . (your feeling, thought, question, etc. about the situation)

O God . . . (your description or name for God in this situation)

I pray . . . (what you want God to do)

(A closing line of expectation or hope)

Invite those who wish to do so to read their Laments aloud, either in groups of 4-6 or to the whole group depending upon group size and time available. (15-20 minutes)

or

Letting a Psalm Speak. Distribute copies of Worksheet A, "Psalm 22." Lead a responsive reading. Then ask each person to circle a line or phrase in the psalm that triggers a particular memory, thought or feeling. Invite participants to talk about the phrase they circled with a partner, someone other than a spouse. (10-15 minutes)

3. **Discussion: God's Intervention.** Read Exodus 2:23-25 aloud again. Speculate as a group: Why does God now hear, see, and respond? What are possible factors that could foster or delay God's intervention? What might such factors suggest about God's partnership with human beings? These are difficult questions. Possible responses might include ideas such as historical circumstances and the readiness of a person or people to hear and respond. Often such factors are only recognizable in hindsight. (10 minutes)

and/or

Hymn Study: God's Response to Human Cries. Many of our hymns illustrate how God hears and responds to human cries for help. Locate as many of the following hymns as you can. Make photocopies of them or list on chalkboard or newsprint the hymns the participants will be able to find in available hymnals.

Abide with Me	God of Grace and God of Glory
Guide Me, O Thy Great Jehovah	I Need Thee Every Hour
Jesus, I Come (Out of My Bondage)	Jesus, Savior, Pilot Me
Lighten the Darkness	My Faith Looks Up to Thee
Nobody Knows the Trouble I've Seen	O God, my God
O God of Earth and Altar	Out of the Depths I Cry to Thee

Distribute hymnals or photocopies of the hymns and copies of Worksheet B, "Cries for Help in Hymns." Divide into groups of 3-5, and assign 3-4 hymns to each group. Have each group work together to do the worksheet. After about 15 minutes, bring the group together. Ask a spokesperson from one group to report on one of the hymns they have studied, inviting others who have studied that hymn to add comments. Invite a spokesperson from a different group to report on a different hymn. Continue reporting in this manner until all the hymns have been discussed. Conclude by observing that the faith expressed in the hymns is often based on *remembering* God's past actions. As Exodus begins, the Hebrew slaves did not seem to have this kind of corporate memory. They could not look back upon the Exodus event! (25 minutes)

4. **Discussion: Words from the Cross.** Read out loud the story of the crucifixion from Matthew 27:27-56. Mention that Jesus' cry from the cross is the first line of Psalm 22. If you did Worksheet A, "Letting a Psalm Speak," invite the group members to turn to that worksheet and to *cry out*, in random order, the line or phrase from the Psalm that they circled. Talk about Jesus' words, "My God, my God, why have you forsaken me?" How do these words make you feel or think about Jesus? About yourself? Conclude this discussion by quoting from the *Resource Book*: "At the very moment one feels compelled to cry out, 'My God, my God, why have you forsaken me?' that person is in the company of Jesus." (15 minutes)

and/or

Responding to the *Resource Book*. Read the following quotation from the *Resource Book* (page 18):

If Jesus was divine, the Son of God, how could he say, "My God, my God, why have you forsaken me?" There is a mystery here that cannot be fully explained, but it is a very important mystery. Christian theology says that Jesus was fully God and fully human. On the cross, then, *God* participated in dying for the sins of others. How could God be godforsaken? Only God knows that, but it becomes gospel for those who now feel themselves to be godforsaken. Jesus' cry from the cross says to them, "I know how you feel. You are not in fact alone. I have been there." Because God was in Christ, that means God knows.

Ask, "What is your reaction to Dr. Gowan's statement?" "How can Jesus' words from the cross be *gospel* (good news) for us?" Again, you may wish to conclude this discussion by quoting the *Resource Book*: "At the very moment one feels compelled to cry out, 'My God, my God, why have you forsaken me?' that person is in the company of Jesus." (10 minutes)

CLOSING

(If you are going to use the "Litany of Lament" as part of the closing, distribute it now, noting that it will not be used until the end of the session.)

1. **Listing Dos and Don'ts.** In the large group, list on chalkboard or newsprint "Dos and Don'ts" to follow during times when one cannot sense the presence of God. Some examples might be:

DO	DON'T
Tell God how you are feeling	Think that God doesn't love you
Read the Psalms	Give up on God (5-10 minutes)

and/or

2. **A Hymn.** Sing or listen to the hymn "O God, My God" (*New Century Hymnal*, United Church Press or GIA Publications). (5 minutes)

or

A Litany. Read responsively the "Litany of Lament." (5 minutes)

and/or

Prayer. Lead the group in closing prayer asking for openness to God's presence. (3 minutes)

Looking Ahead

One of the suggestions for *Exploring the Scripture* for the next session requires asking a volunteer to make a brief report on the meaning of YHWH. Select a volunteer. You may want to suggest that in addition to reading the information in the *Resource Book*, he or she may want to read *Theology in Exodus,* pp. 80-87.

Psalm 22

My God, my God, why have you forsaken me?

    Why are you so far from helping me, from the words of my groaning?

O my God, I cry by day, but you do not answer;

    And by night, but find no rest.

Yet you are holy,

    Enthroned on the praises of Israel.

In you our ancestors trusted; . . .

To you they cried, and were saved; . . .

But I am a worm, and not human;

    Scorned by others, and despised by the people. . . .

I am poured out like water,

    and all my bones are out of joint; . . .

For dogs arc all around me;

    a company of evildoers encircles me. . . .

But you, O Lord, do not be far away!

    O my help, come quickly to my aid!

Deliver my soul from the sword,

    my life from the power of the dog! . . .

From you comes my praise in the great congregation;

    my vows I will pay before those who fear him.

The poor shall eat and be satisfied;

    those who seek him shall praise the Lord.

Cries for Help in Hymns

HYMN TITLE

What problems or needs are mentioned?

What does the hymn suggest for us to do?

What assurances or hope does the hymn offer?

Litany of Lament

O God, the Hebrew slaves in Egypt groaned and cried for help.

    At times, we also groan and cry for help.   Exodus 2:23

Then I remember also these words of the Psalmist

"Be still before the LORD and wait patiently,

The salvation of the righteous is from the LORD.

God rescues them and saves them

because they take refuge in God.   Psalm 37:7,40

At times, O God, we cry with the Psalmist,

How long, O LORD?

    Do not be silent; do not be far from me!"   Psalm 35:17,22

Yet the Psalmist also said,

"LORD, what do I wait for?

    My hope is in you.   Psalm 39:7

At times, O God, we wonder with Isaiah,

"Where is the God who brought the Hebrew slaves up out of the sea?

Where are your zeal and might?

    Where is your compassion?"   Isaiah 63:11,15

Yet Isaiah also said

"They who wait for the LORD shall renew their strength,

they shall mount up with wings like eagles,

they shall run and not be weary,

    they shall walk and not faint.   Isaiah 40:31

At times, O God, we feel, as Job did,

"If I go forward, you are not there;

Or backward, I cannot perceive you.

On the left you hide,

    I turn to the right, but I cannot see you."   Job 23:8-9

Then I take comfort in these words of Paul,

"I am sure that neither death, nor life, nor angels, nor principalities,

nor things present, nor things to come, nor powers, nor height, nor depth,

nor anything else in all creation, will be able to separate us from the

love of God in Christ Jesus our LORD.   Romans 8:38

At times, we might even feel like uttering the words Jesus cried from the cross,

"My God, my God, why have you forsaken me?   Mark 15:34

I trust these words of Jesus,

"Lo, I am with you always,

even to the end of the age."   Matthew 28:20

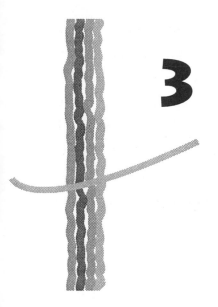

3

THE BURNING BUSH: GOD'S SELF-INTRODUCTION

Background from the Author

Chapters 4 and 5 of *Theology in Exodus* will provide additional resources for this session. You will note that I have not tried to include the topics found in chapters 2 and 3, since that would overload your work at this point in the course. Later sessions will refer you to some of the material in these chapters.

Some discussion of the importance of names in our own culture may be helpful at the beginning of the session. For the most part, we tend to use names as rather arbitrary labels. Consider the way companies change their names; e.g. from American Oil Company to Amoco, or from U. S. Steel to USX. So, I have focused on personal names, since one's own name and the names of loved ones do have a remarkable power over us. This helps us to understand the importance of names in the Bible and the ways the word "name" itself is used.

The name "Jehovah" may come up in your discussion. I did not deal with that in the *Resource Book*, for unless one knows Hebrew the explanation can be a bit confusing. If it comes up, you should be ready with the following information: It is a strange combination of the consonants of one word with the vowels of another, so is not a valid representation of the name of God in the Old Testament. It came into existence in this way: The consonants in the Hebrew text are represented in English as YHWH, but in European languages, such as German, they are JHVH. You will see that this spelling accounts for part of the word Jehovah. During the post-exilic period, Jews began substituting the word *Adonay* ("Lord") for Yahweh when they read the scriptures. During the Christian era, when marks to indicate the vowels were added to the biblical manuscripts, the vowels for Adonay were added to YHWH to remind readers, "Don't say Yahweh; say Adonay." Christian scholars who learned Hebrew in early times did not realize that and thought the consonants of *JaHVeH* and the vowels of *Adonay* really belonged together. The first vowel is a super-short "a," which they took as "e." Thus: J-e-H-o-V-a-H. Now you see why I did not include all this in the *Resource Book*. It may or may not be helpful. In sum, don't use Jehovah.

The point about partial fulfillment of promises may need further emphasis, for there is a fairly strong tendency to think that unless a promise is fulfilled completely, it isn't fulfilled. That is not the way it works in the Bible, however. Many books and articles that deal with promise will label the Old Testament a book of promise and the New as a book of fulfillment. This can be misleading, for the Old Testament already speaks of fulfillments, and the New Testament contains promises that still have not come to perfection. This is the point in the course where we might have dealt with eschatology—the predictions in the prophetic books of the days to come when God will make everything right. If members of the group wonder about the absence of that material, the reason is that Exodus does not contain any such passages, and we have enough to do, just dealing with the themes it introduces. The theme of hope, which is a major aspect of eschatology, appears from Genesis on, so that does appear in my discussion of promise.

SESSION PLANS

Learning Objectives

This session is intended to enable participants to:

1. Cite personal examples of the importance of names.

2. Identify some possible meanings associated with the divine name.

3. Discuss the tension between promise and fulfillment in the Bible.

4. Express thankfulness for God's promise of continued presence.

Resources You May Need

Chalkboard or newsprint and markers

Bibles for each participant

3 Bibles of the same translation or 3 copies of Exodus 3:1-15

Copies of the worksheet "Promise and Fulfillment" and the litany "I Will Be with You"

Leadership Strategy

SETTING THE STAGE

1. **Naming God in Prayer.** As you begin this session which focuses on the revelation of the divine name, ask members of the group, "What are some names we use to address God?" List their suggestions on chalkboard or newsprint. The list may include "Yahweh, Rock, Father, Mother, Friend, Savior, Holy One," etc. Invite people to look at the list and say why they prefer particular names. After a few minutes, pray the following prayer:

    > O God, (read their list of names for God), thank you for the many names we can use to address you and for all the meanings these names convey to us about who you are and about who you are to us. As you drew near to Moses and promised, "I will be with you," draw near to us, please, and be with us as we gather in your name to study your word. Amen. (5 minutes)

    or

    Prayer from the Psalms. Read Psalm 9:1-2,9-10. If you want the group to read the Psalm together, photocopy it from "Prayers from the Psalms" in the Appendix.

    or

    Opening Prayer. Pray in your own words asking God to be with the group as you study together. (3 minutes)

2. **Telling Stories about Names.** In groups of 3 or 4, ask participants to tell brief stories about their names (any of their names—first, middle, last, maiden, nickname). The story might be about how they got the name, who they are named for, what the name means, how they feel about the name, etc. (10-15 minutes)

and/or

Discussion: Importance of Names. Lead a short discussion about the importance of names.

- Do they agree with Dale Carnegie's statement quoted in the *Resource Book* that "a person's name is the sweetest, most important sound in the English language"?

- Why are names so important to us?

- What does it say to you when someone calls you by your name? (10 minutes)

EXPLORING THE SCRIPTURE

1. **Reading the Scripture.** Read Exodus 3:1-15 as a dialogue, asking 3 volunteers to act as Narrator, Moses and the LORD. Have 3 Bibles of the same translation available, or photocopy the passage so that all the participants will read from the same version. Then read or state in your own words this information from the *Resource Book*:

   This passage is usually referred to as "the call of Moses," and that is an important part of the contents of these chapters. We will read them that way in the next session. There is something else going on here, however, which is not noticed as often. When Moses asks God, "Who am I that I should go to Pharaoh?", the discussion that follows is not about Moses; it is about God and who God is. Eventually Moses' qualifications will come into the picture. But first, Moses needs to learn about God. (10 minutes)

2. **Introducing God's Name.** Write "YHWH" on chalkboard or newsprint. Summarize Dr. Gowan's explanation of the use of YHWH and Yahweh in the section of the *Resource Book* titled "The God of Israel has a name: Yahweh." Include the following points:

- how YHWH became "Yahweh"

- possible meanings of "Yahweh" (summarize very briefly)

- how YHWH is translated in most English Bibles (LORD). (10 minutes)

or

A report. Ahead of time, ask a volunteer to make a brief report on the meaning of YHWH, based on the information in the *Resource Book.*

and

Discussion. Ask, "How did knowing God's name seem to change the relationship between Yahweh and the people of Israel?" In leading the discussion, use information from the sections "Why Did God Need an Introduction?" and "The God of Israel Has a New Name: Yahweh" in the *Resource Book.* Note particularly that at the beginning of Exodus, the people seem to know little about their past and may not have known of God's promise to Abraham and Sarah. Personal relationship with God seems missing; Exodus 2:23 does not even say they cried out to God, just that they cried out. Conclude with Dr. Gowan's statement at the end of the section "The God of Israel Has a Name: Yahweh": "When God gave Israel a name by which to address God, the people were assured there was something at work that was more than a 'force' or an ideal. God was revealed as a person who can be addressed by name." (5-10 minutes)

3. **God's Name in Later Scripture.** Ask volunteers to read aloud the following passages. As each passage is read, ask the group, "What does the divine name seem to represent in this passage?" Write their answers on chalkboard or newsprint.

   Psalm 20:1

   Isaiah 30:27-28

   Matthew 6:9

   Philippians 2:5-11

Summarize by noting that in these passages God's *name* represents the very identity of God or Christ. Give some examples to clarify this statement.

To honor God's name is to honor God.

To heal in Christ's name is to heal with Christ's power.

To pray in Christ's name is to offer a prayer that is in harmony with all Christ represented and taught. (20 minutes)

or

Telling Who God Is. Working individually or in groups of 3-4, ask the group members to imagine that God sent them to appear before a congressional subcommittee on health care to demand adequate health insurance coverage for all. The government official asks, "Who is this God who sent you?" They are to answer by finishing the following sentence in as many different ways as they can. Write the sentence on chalkboard or newsprint.

Our God is the One who _____

After about 5 minutes, ask the group to call out some of their sentence completions. (10 minutes)

4. **The Tension between Promise and Fulfillment.** God's words to Moses from the burning bush contain a promise: "I have observed the misery of my people who are in Egypt: I have heard their cry on account of their taskmasters. Indeed I know their sufferings, and I have come down to deliver them from the Egyptians." (3:7-8). Yahweh is a God who makes promises. In groups of 3-7, reflect on the tension between promise and fulfillment by doing the worksheet "Promise and Fulfillment." After about 20 minutes, bring the whole group together and have spokespersons from each group read the faith statement written by their groups. (30 minutes)

or

Living with Unfulfilled Promises. Read aloud Exodus 6:2-8. Then ask, "What parts of this promise have been fulfilled? What is yet to be fulfilled?" Write their responses on chalkboard or newsprint. The section "Standing on the Promises" will be helpful as you lead this discussion.

Then read aloud Romans 6:3-11. Ask the participants to think quietly about the tension between the reality of our lives and Paul's promise that in Christ we die to sin. Then ask, "What should our actions and attitude be when God's promises seem to be unfulfilled?" Guide the discussion to bring out the following points from the section "Jesus as the Fulfillment of God's Promises" in the *Resource Book*:

- The tension between promise and fulfillment continues in the New Testament.

- Radical change *is* possible through faith in Christ, but no one is yet perfect.

- Although fulfillments are not complete in this life, God's promises are evidence that God is indeed faithful, and is at work to make them complete one day.

- We live in gratitude and faithfulness for what God has already done and in the hope for the perfection that is to come. (15 minutes)

<u>CLOSING</u>

A Litany. Read responsively the Litany, "I Will Be with You." (5 minutes)

or

A Scripture Reading. Read 1 Corinthians 13:9-13. (3 minutes)

and/or

Prayer. Offer a prayer of thanksgiving for God's promise, "I will be with you," and for God's faithfulness. (3 minutes)

Looking Ahead

An option for Session 4 suggests asking a volunteer to present a 3-5-minute report on ordination procedures for your denomination. If you choose this option, ask your minister for a copy of this information and give it to the volunteer.

Locate the hymn "Here I Am, Lord" if you wish to use it as a closing in the next session. You might ask a good vocalist from your choir to prerecord it for you.

Promise and Fulfillment

1. Read aloud one of the following passages:

Group A: Exodus 6:2-8

Group B: Ezekiel 36:26-28

Group C: Romans 6:3-11

2. Talk about these questions :

- What promise is given in the passage you read?

- How has this promise begun to be fulfilled?

- What is yet to be fulfilled?

- What should our attitude and actions be when promises are unfulfilled?

3. As a group, write a faith statement by completing the following sentences:

God promises

We will

We trust that

Litany: "I Will Be with You"

When our ancestor Jacob was running away from the righteous anger of the brother he had cheated, God stood beside Jacob in the middle of the night and said, "I am with you."

Remind us, Gracious God, that no matter what we have done, you love us and come to us and grant us new beginnings.

When Moses asked Yahweh, "Who am I that I should go to Pharaoh and bring the Israelites out of Egypt"? Yahweh answered, "I will be with you."

God of power and might, help us to venture into the scary and unknown places to which you call us, knowing that you are with us.

When God warned the prophet Jeremiah about disaster that would come to the people of Israel, God said, "They will fight against you, but they shall not prevail against you, for I am with you."

O Companion and Friend, support us with your presence in all our battles, whether our adversaries are injustice, poor health, temptation, disappointment, or our own failures.

When God spoke to the people of Israel in exile in Babylon, God said, "Do not fear. . . I have called you by name, you are mine. When you pass through the waters, I will be with you."

In the tough times of life, help us to trust you.

Matthew spoke of the fulfillment of prophecy: "Look, the virgin shall conceive and bear a son, and they shall name him Emmanuel, which means, 'God is with us.'"

O come, O come, Emmanuel!

The risen Christ left his disciples with these words: "I am with you always, to the end of the age."

Thank you, O God, for your promise to be with us! Amen.

. . . . based on Exodus 3:11-12; Genesis 28:15; Jeremiah 1:19; Isaiah 43:1-2; Matthew 1:23; 28:20.

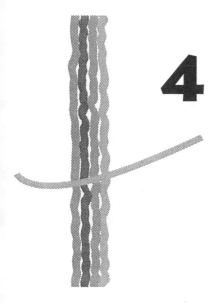

4 MOSES: AN UNLIKELY LEADER

Background from the Author

You will notice that this session moves rather quickly from Moses as the classic example of leadership to the various forms of ministry carried out by Christians in the early church. That seemed to be more useful for the purposes of this course than providing details about kings, priests, prophets, and wise men in ancient Israel.

Discussions may vary considerably from one group to another, when leadership is the topic. In one group the issues surrounding leaders may be a lively subject, and some of the problems faced by Moses may be relevant. Unfortunately, that may also be a very touchy subject, so if you anticipate it, think about how to handle it with care.

It probably will be helpful for you to have at hand information on the form of government used in your denomination and its procedures for ordination, for there may be questions about the relationship between church polity and the New Testament.

In some groups, spiritual gifts may become the principal subject of interest. This also can be a sensitive subject at times. If you anticipate that, it may be because for some the subject is nearly confined to gifts of healing and of speaking in tongues. 1 Corinthians 12-14 is an important passage for two reasons. It puts speaking in tongues in its proper place, as only one among many gifts, and that may be relevant for some groups. Important for every group is its extensive listing of gifts, all of which come from the Spirit and all of which are needed for the work of Christ. This is a subject which has probably been neglected in many congregations. One or more good commentaries on 1 Corinthians may be helpful as you consider these chapters.

Remembering the study of the name of God in the previous session, some participants may be puzzled by the capitalization of GOD, rather than Lord, in three texts that are quoted in this session, Ezekiel 2:4; 3:8-11; and Jeremiah 1:6. If you are asked, it is to be explained in this way: In each case, the prophet is saying in Hebrew, *Adonay Yahweh*, i.e. "LORD Yahweh." But now the translator is in a trap. Following Jewish tradition, he has substituted LORD for Yahweh, and he scarcely wants to say "LORD LORD." So, in desperation, he uses "LORD GOD," where the capitalized GOD really stands for Yahweh.

Since the participants will have read Exodus 4:24-26 in preparation for this session, they will certainly be puzzled by it and will wonder why I said nothing about it. The reasons are that it did not fit the theme of leadership and that there is no useful theological conclusion we can draw from it. But it will almost certainly come up, with a request for an explanation. Childs' commentary on Exodus will share all the difficulties with you, and it is recommended as the best we can do with an extremely difficult passage. If possible, try not to spend too much of your time on this, since no one is certain what it means.

The section on Jethro introduces Exodus 18 out of order, but it seemed necessary to do so. You may want to consult Session 8 as you prepare, since I take up the chapter again there and may have answered questions that will come up in this session.

Careful readers will notice that 6:2-13 parallels 3:7-17 in many respects. It seems that God revealed the divine name to Moses twice. Notice that the continuity is not smooth in this area, also. There is much in 6:2-7:5 that reminds us of chapters 3-4. It may be that there were two slightly different recollections of the appointment of Moses present within Israel, and they have both been included.

Several important themes that first appear in these chapters are developed in the next session, so the group needs to be patient. They are the hardening of Pharaoh's heart (4:21), Israel as God's first-born (4:22—Session 6), and "You shall know that I am the LORD" (6:7).

SESSION PLANS

Learning Objectives

This session is intended to enable participants to:

1. Outline the pattern of typical Biblical call stories.

2. Describe their own sense of call.

3. Identify qualities needed for church leadership.

4. Name some of their own spiritual gifts.

Resources You May Need

Bibles

Chalkboard or newsprint and markers

Typing paper, small stickers that can be written on

Hymnals containing "Here I Am, Lord" and/or tape player and prerecorded tape of the hymn

Copies of the following: Worksheet A "The Pattern of Biblical Call Narratives," Worksheet B "Finding Yourself in the Story," the litany "God's Word to Moses and to Us," and Worksheet A (from Session 5) "Ten Plagues" (preparation for the next session)

Leadership Strategy

<u>SETTING THE STAGE</u>

1. **Prayer from the Psalms.** Read Psalm 67:1-2. If you want the group to read the Psalm together, photocopy it from "Prayers from the Psalms" in the Appendix.

and/or

Opening Prayer. Offer your own prayer giving thanks for God's call to women and men in all times who have led us into the presence of God. (3 minutes)

Introducing Moses and Pharaoh. Introduce today's theme as leadership, then and now. Divide into groups of 3-4. Give each group one of the following assignments which you have printed on typing paper or newsprint. You may need to give the same assignment to more than one group, depending on the number of participants.

A: Read Exodus 1:8-22. You have been asked to write a Letter of Reference for Pharaoh, who has applied for a job as City Administrator. Discuss his leadership skills, style, effectiveness, etc. and write the letter.

B: Read Exodus 2:1-10. Discuss the events that have taken place. Prepare a "60 Minutes" type investigative report on this story or write a news story covering these events.

C: Read Exodus 2:11-22. Moses has applied for a leadership study grant from Harvard University. You have been asked to write a character reference. Who is this person? What makes him tick? What are his prospects? Write the reference.

Bring the group together and have a representative from each group present a report. (15-20 minutes)

or

Review. Review the action of the last two sessions by asking, "What was the situation of the Israelites when we left them the last time we met?" Guide the discussion to bring out the following points:

- In Egypt, a Pharaoh who no longer remembered Joseph made the Hebrew people slaves.

- Egyptian policies became more and more oppressive.

- The Hebrew people had no leader other than their Egyptian taskmasters.

- Moses, who seemed groomed for leadership because of his Hebrew birth and Egyptian education, had killed a man and fled to Midian.

- The people groaned and cried, but did not seem to sense a personal God.

- Finally, God spoke to Moses from a burning bush, saying, "I am the God of your father, the God of Abraham, the God of Isaac, and the God of Jacob." (5 minutes)

EXPLORING THE SCRIPTURE

1. **Introducing the Concept of Call.** In the large group, introduce the concept of "call" using information from the *Resource Book* section, "Someone Has to Lead." Note particularly the importance of leadership and the variety of ways leaders attain their position (e.g., strength, power, heredity, democratic election). Then ask:

- What constitutes a call?

- Whom does God call?

- What does God call people to do?

Invite examples as these questions are discussed. Conclude this introductory discussion by noting that three dynamics are often intermingled in a call: (1) a need, (2) one's personal sense of direction from God, and (3) the community's validation of the call by accepting one's leadership. (5 minutes)

and

Examining Moses' Call. Give each person a copy of the worksheet "The Pattern of Biblical Call Narratives." Lead the group through a review of the call of Moses in Exodus 3:1-4:17 and fill out the worksheet together. What insights can the group identify about the way God works through people to bring about change? (10-15 minutes)

or

Comparing Call Stories. Give each person a copy of Worksheet A, "The Pattern of Biblical Call Narratives," which outlines the common pattern of several biblical call experiences. Divide into groups of 3-5 to examine one of the following call stories in the Bible and to fill out the worksheet. Smaller groups need not use every passage.

Exodus 3:1-4:17	The Call of Moses
Judges 6:11-24	The Call of Gideon
Isaiah 6:1-9	The Call of Isaiah
Jeremiah 1:4-10	The Call of Jeremiah
Ezekiel 2:3-11	The Call of Ezekiel

Have a representative from each group summarize that group's observations. (20-30 minutes)

2. **Finding Yourself in the Story.** The chapters of Exodus we have read thus far show a variety of ways that people can respond to an adverse situation. The responses range from the negative leadership of Pharaoh to the passive acceptance of the Hebrew people to the strong positive leadership of Moses. Invite the group to talk briefly about the different roles played by the following characters mentioned in Exodus 5.

The Egyptian Taskmasters

The Hebrew Foremen

The Hebrew Slaves

Pharaoh

Moses

Aaron

Then hand out copies of worksheet B "Finding Yourself in the Story." Invite group members to complete the sheet, working individually, and then to talk about it with persons sitting close to them. (20 minutes)

or

Telling Personal Stories. In pairs, invite group members to tell about a time when they felt *called* to do, say, or write something. (The word *call* may sound too forbidding for some to claim, so include other words such as *driven* or *compelled*.) Ask the participants to describe their sense of being called (driven, urged, or pulled) and to tell how it felt to respond or not to respond. (10 minutes)

3. **Report on Ordination Credentials.** Ahead of time, ask a volunteer to prepare a report on ordination procedures in your denomination. After the report is presented, ask the group members to make a list of the qualifications and characteristics they think are most important for ordained ministers to have. Then ask, "Which of the qualities we listed did Moses seem to have?" Some discussion may arise as they answer this question. For example, some may question whether a person who kills someone and runs away has *integrity*. And so far Moses has not demonstrated many *leadership skills*. Conclude this discussion by inviting the group members to add to their original list. For example, they may now want to list "willingness to change," "receptiveness to God's leading," or "trust in God's power." (10-15 minutes)

Setting Standards for Clergy. Read Acts 1:15-26. Referring to the section "God Knows, But How Do We Know?" in the *Resource Book*, discuss how the story of Matthias' selection for a position of leadership reflects the three dynamics of a call addressed in Exploring 1 above. If the group shared a report on ordination credentials ask, "How does the selection of Matthias compare to that ordination process? What elements are the same and what are different?" (10 minutes)

or

Naming our Role Models. Introduce the activity by mentioning that our study of the call of Moses as a leader of the Hebrews invites us to think about qualities of leadership in our own church communities. Invite group members to think of a particular church leader they have known and admired. In pairs, have participants share their answers to these questions:

• What made that leader an admirable model?

• How did he/she handle difficult situations?

• What was his or her greatest contribution to the church?

• How does his or her sense of *call* seem similar to or different from Moses' call?   (5 minutes)

or

Commandments for Supporting Church Leaders. Invite the group to brainstorm answers to the question, "How can we support leaders in our local churches?" Record their ideas on chalkboard or newsprint. Then develop a list of "Five Commandments for Supporting Church Leaders." (If your group is large you may wish to subdivide into smaller groups to do this and then compare the resulting lists.) (10-15 minutes)

4. **Identifying Gifts.** In groups of 3-4, invite the participants to recall and tell about three things they have done that gave them great satisfaction. One person at a time will tell his or her three stories while the others listen to discern the "gifts" they perceive being used in these accomplishments. The listeners may

make notes and ask clarifying questions, but should refrain from interrupting or commenting. When the speaker has finished, all the listeners are to write 3-5 gifts they have discerned through listening to these stories, writing each on a separate sticker. Each listener, in turn, then "showers" the speaker with gifts by sticking them on the speaker's clothing. The next person then shares three stories and receives the "shower" until each person has had a turn to speak.

Bring the group together. Ask:

- How are gifts recognized and nurtured?

- How and where do we share our gifts?

- What holds us back from sharing them? (30 minutes)

and/or

Discussing Gifts. Read 1 Corinthians 12 silently. On chalkboard or newsprint, have the group make a list of the gifts named in this passage. Then have the group add specific gifts that contribute to the Body of their own church. Ask:

- How are these gifts called forth?

- How are they inhibited?

- How can we encourage the development of gifts in our congregation? (10 minutes)

and/or

Writing about a Gift. Have each person pick one of the gifts listed above. Invite them each to write a brief statement of praise for the gift similar to the way Paul described the gift of love in 1 Corinthians 13. Write a suggested outline on chalkboard or newsprint:

(The gift) is_____.

(The gift) is not_____.

(A concluding statement about the gift)_____.

You may wish to make this an optional "homework" assignment. If you complete the activity during this session, invite those who wish to do so to read their Praise for a Gift to the group. (20 minutes)

<u>CLOSING</u>

A Litany. Read responsively the Litany, "God's Word to Moses and to Us." (3 minutes)

and/or

A Hymn. Sing or listen to the hymn, "Here I Am, Lord." If possible, have one person sing the verses with all joining in the chorus. (5 minutes)

and/or

Prayer. Conclude with a brief prayer asking God to bless and nurture all our gifts and to grant the grace and courage to share them.

Looking Ahead

The next session (Exploring the Scripture) asks participants to fill out a worksheet, "10 Plagues," as they read the chapter and scripture assignment. If you choose this option, you will need to distribute this worksheet at the end of this session.

Exploring the Scripture suggests asking 10 volunteers to prepare to tell the story of one of the plagues in their own words. If you choose this option, print Scripture assignments listed on 3 x 5 cards and give them to the volunteers. You will find these verses listed on the worksheet for Session 5.

Session 6 suggests celebrating a Seder meal and/or inviting a rabbi to talk with the group. Look ahead to this session now so that you can begin gathering the materials needed. If you have invited a rabbi, you may want to confirm the details of that visit this week. If you decide to have a potluck meal for Session 6, you will need to begin making plans at this session.

The Pattern of Biblical Call Narratives

THE THEOPHANY: (An encounter with the divine) What was seen and heard?

THE COMMISSION: What does God ask of the one being called?

OBJECTIONS: What concerns are expressed?

DIVINE REJOINDER: How does God respond to the objections?

CLOSING/SIGN: How does the encounter conclude?

Finding Yourself in the Story

Think for a few minutes:

      a. Where do you see change needed or happening today?

      b. What is your position with regard to this situation?

Then complete the following statement:

WHEN (Describe a particular event or situation where change is needed or taking place):

I FEEL LIKE (Circle one)

an Egyptian taskmaster	a Hebrew supervisor	Pharaoh
a Hebrew slave	Moses	Aaron

BECAUSE:

Litany: God's Words to Moses and to Us

God said to Moses from the burning bush, "Moses, Moses."   (Exodus 3:4)

Help us, God to hear you when you speak to us, and to say as Moses did, "Here I am."

God said, "Take off your sandals, for the place where you are standing is holy ground."
                                                                           (Exodus 3:5)

Remind us, O God, that wherever you meet us, that is a holy place.

God said, "I have seen how cruelly my people are being treated in Egypt; I have heard them cry out to be rescued."   (Exodus 3:7)

May we see through your eyes, the needs of people to be rescued and may we be willing to respond to their cry.

God said, "I am sending you so that you can lead my people."   (Exodus 3:10)

We are overwhelmed by the immensity of the task that you place before us; give us strength and wisdom, O God, sufficient for the task.

God said, "I AM WHO I AM. That is my name forever; this is what all future generations will call me."   (Exodus 3:14, 15)

Thank you, God, for revealing to us your name and yourself, so that we may know you as the One who delivers all who call upon you.

God said, "Now go! I will help you speak and will teach you what to say. (Exodus 4:12)

Teach us to hear, O God, and help us to respond.

From *Meeting God in the Bible*, by Donald L. Griggs (The Kerygma Program, 1992) p. 64.

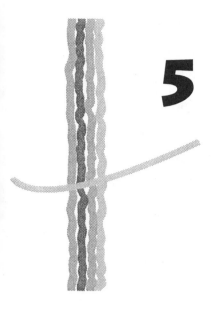

5 THE PLAGUES: WHO IS GOD— YAHWEH OR PHARAOH?

Background from the Author

Some writers of liberation theology have found Exodus to be very useful, because of its message concerning God's intervention into human history on behalf of the weak over against the rich and powerful. This leads to questions about the point with which the session begins, that the sins of Egypt and the suffering of the Hebrews fall into the background in the story of the plagues. My point is not to suggest God's concern for justice for the weak is unimportant. It is present in the early chapters of Exodus, and throughout the rest of the Bible, but recognizing the change of emphasis is important for a good understanding of the plagues.

If you read all of Chapter 6 of *Theology in Exodus*, you will note that this session does not take up the theme of the divine destroyer in the way the book does. It is not an easy theme to work with, and had to be discussed at considerable length in the book. For this course I recognized that the subject of the hardening of Pharaoh's heart had to be considered, for it is a perennial problem for readers of the Bible. Since I found that knowledge of God was one of the keys to the meaning of the plague narrative, I decided that idea should be emphasized and the difficult subject of natural disasters left to one side.

There may be questions about historical evidence for the plagues. In the first Session 1 acknowledged that there is nothing that reflects these events in the rather extensive records we have for the history of ancient Egypt. Two comments may be added. Kings liked to record their victories on monuments for all to see, not their defeats. It would not be likely that there would be a public record of the loss of an army in the Sea. However, it seems that an environmental disaster as extensive as the plagues should have left some evidence in the records of daily life preserved in Egypt. The second comment takes the form of a question. Could it be that the effects of the plagues were not that extensive on Egypt, after all, but that the escape from Egypt had such a profound effect on Israel that they told the story in an extravagant way in order to reveal what that event really meant to them? We cannot know the answer to that question, of course, since we were not there.

Exodus is written in order to show movement on God's part. God is not there in the first two chapters. Then God is introduced in an impressive way, in Chapters 3-4. In this session, we see the theme "Then you will know that I am Yahweh" running through the plague narrative. God desires to be known, and it is important to emphasize that "knowledge" is not merely intellectual but experiential—leading to a relationship. When the people reach Sinai, God's desire to be very near the people is emphasized in the making of the covenant relationship and the building of the tabernacle. Your group may get bogged down in all the destruction recorded in these chapters, so it will be important to emphasize this movement, of which God's desire to be known and to be near is an essential step.

SESSION PLANS

Learning Objectives

This session is intended to enable participants to:

1. Tell the story of the contest between Yahweh and the Pharaoh.

2. Suggest one or more possible interpretations of the statement that God hardened Pharaoh's heart.

3. Name some ways we know God in our own lives.

4. Express thanks or praise for the power of the One God.

Resources You May Need

Extra copies of Worksheet A, "10 Plagues," for any who may not have received it last session

Chalkboard or newsprint and markers

Hymnals containing the hymn, "Go Down Moses"

Copies of Worksheet B, "Knowing God"

Leadership Strategy

SETTING THE STAGE

1. **Prayer from the Psalms.** Read aloud together Psalm 46:8-11. If you want the group to read the Psalm together, photocopy it from "Prayers from the Psalms" in the Appendix. (3 minutes)

and/or

A Psalm Meditation. Invite the group to repeat silently, over and over, the line from Psalm 46: "Be still and know that I am God." (3 minutes)

or

Opening Prayer. Offer a prayer asking that this time of study and reflection may lead to a deeper knowledge of God. (3 minutes)

2. **"Homework."** If you assigned optional "homework" from the last session, invite those who wish to do so to read their statements of praise for a spiritual gift. (5 minutes)

EXPLORING THE SCRIPTURE

1. **Reviewing the Plagues.** As a group, briefly tell the story of the plagues using the information on the "Ten Plagues" worksheet. (You distributed this worksheet at the conclusion of Session 4 and asked participants to fill it out as they read this week's lesson.) Write the headings on newsprint or chalkboard:

PLAGUE #   PLAGUE   YAHWEH'S WORDS   PHARAOH'S RESPONSE

As group members call out information, write key words or phrases in the appropriate place on the chart. After the information is complete, invite group members to note similarities in the pattern of the stories. (10 minutes)

or

Retelling the Plague Stories. Assign each plague to individuals or pairs, using the Scripture references listed in Worksheet A, "10 Plagues," and ask the persons or pairs to prepare to tell the story briefly in their own words, being sure to include what Yahweh and Pharaoh said. After about 10 minutes, begin the story-telling, asking the group to think of themselves as telling stories around a campfire. After the stories are told, ask, "What words did the Pharaoh say again and again in these stories? What words did God say repeatedly?" (20-25 minutes)

or

Reports on the Plagues. Ahead of time, make the above assignment to 10 volunteers, asking each to tell the story of one of the plagues. After the last report, invite group members to note similarities in the pattern of the plague stories and in the words spoken by the Pharaoh and God. (15 minutes)

Raising Troubling Issues. Ask volunteers to read aloud 7:3, 9:12, and 10:1-2 to the group. Ask, "What troubles you about the statement that God hardened Pharaoh's heart?" Invite them to discuss their concerns briefly by asking why these are troubling issues. Do not try to "solve" these problems; the purpose of this activity is simply to allow them to express their questions and concerns. (10-15 minutes)

and

Discussing the Hardening of Pharaoh's Heart. Quote Dr. Gowan's statements in the *Resource Book* about the hardening of Pharaoh's heart:

Readers of the book of Exodus are troubled by the statements in the plague narrative that say God hardened the Pharaoh's heart . . . It seems to mean it was God who made it impossible for the Pharaoh to do the right thing . . . That refusal, which thus seems not to be the Pharaoh's fault, then led to the terrible disasters we have just been reviewing. This seems completely unfair, and not in keeping with anything the Bible says about God elsewhere.

Then read aloud Romans 9:14-18. Summarize the key ideas from the section "A Difficult Problem—the Hardening of Pharaoh's Heart" in the *Resource Book*. Include the following thoughts:

- The way God dealt with the Pharaoh in the plagues is not to be taken as an example of the way God always deals with people; it is a unique case. To support this idea, read aloud Ezekiel 18:30-32, noting that God wants people to "turn, then, and live."

- The story of the plagues does not take freeing the slaves as its primary focus.

- The hardening of the heart must be a part of the contest between the true God and the one who thought he was god. (10 minutes)

3. **Debate: Who Is God?** Plan strategies for the contest between Yahweh and the Pharaoh. On newsprint or chalkboard, write the following:

HOW WILL WE PROVE THAT PHARAOH/YAHWEH IS GOD?

- What must happen?

- What about compromise?

- What must the defeated opponent's attitude be?

Divide the group into two sections. Members of one section are to imagine they are *Moses*; members of the other section are to be *Pharaoh*. If the sections are larger than 6, subdivide each section into teams of 3-6 to discuss the questions and plan their strategy. After about 15 minutes, bring the whole group together. Ask a volunteer from each section (or each team if you have sub-divided into teams) to present strategies to the whole group, inviting others from that section or team to contribute additional suggestions. (30 minutes)

or

Discussion of God's Purpose. Lead a discussion with the whole group about God's purpose for causing the plagues. Ask, "Why might the Hebrew slaves have believed that the Pharaoh was the true God? What did Yahweh say about the reason for the plagues?" For help in answering these questions, encourage the group members to recall the discussion from Exploring the Scripture 1. They may also want to look up Exodus 5:1-2; 8:10; 9:13-14; 10:1-2; 11:7-8. (10 minutes)

4. **Personal Reflection: Knowing God.** The question of how we know God is as relevant today as it was in Moses' time. In groups of 4-6, discuss the questions on Worksheet B, "Knowing God." After 20-25 minutes, bring the group together. List the different words and phrases participants suggest as substitutes for the word *know* on newsprint or chalkboard. Then list ways that knowing God makes a difference in our lives. (30-35 minutes)

or

Research and Prayer. Ask volunteers to look up and read aloud Exodus 5:1-2 and 9:13-14. Ask, "How do these passages suggest that the Israelites and Egyptians will *know* God? How else do we *know* God?" Conclude the discussion by reading aloud John 1:14-18. Then invite each person to write a brief prayer to finish the following sentence:

O God, I know you (by/when/in) _____.　(20 minutes)

CLOSING

1. **Sentence Prayers.** If group members have written prayers (Exploring 4), invite them to offer these prayers. Because some may not wish to pray aloud, invite them to offer their prayers as the spirit moves them (rather than speaking in turn around a circle) and suggest that prayers may also be offered silently. (5-10 minutes)

and/or

A Hymn. Sing the hymn, "Go Down, Moses." (3 minutes)

and/or

A Litany. Read Psalm 105 as a litany. Use verses 1-2 as a refrain which the whole group reads at the beginning, and after each of the following assigned "solo readings:"

1) verses 23-25

2) verses 26-32

3) verses 33-38

4) verses 43-45. (5 minutes)

Looking Ahead

The next session (Exploring 1) suggests celebrating a Seder meal and/or inviting a Jewish Rabbi to talk with the group. If you plan to include one of the options for a meal (bag lunches, potluck, cooked by a committee), finalize the plans for this event. If you plan to usc the simpler liturgical celebration, collect the necessary supplies. You may want to ask 3-4 volunteers to bring some of the food and table appointments and to come early to set up.

The next session (Exploring 2) also asks the group to compare your communion liturgy to the Passover Seder. Copies of your communion liturgy may be printed in your hymnal. Or ask your minister for a copy.

Session 7 (Exploring 1) suggests showing a segment of the video, "The Ten Commandments." If you want to use this option, ask the group if anyone owns this video or knows someone who does. If not, you may want to reserve this video at a video rental store in your area.

Ten Plagues

Passage	Plague #	Plague	Yahweh's Words	Pharaoh's Response
7:14-25	1			
8:1-15	2			
8:16-19	3			
8:20-32	4			
9:1-7	5			
9:8-12	6			
9:13-35	7			
10:1-20	8			
10:21-29	9			
11:1-10	10			

Knowing God

Look up the following passages:

- Exodus 5:1-2

- Exodus 9:14

- Psalm 46:8-11

- John 1:14-18

- Matthew 26:72

In each passage, what words or phrases might you substitute for the word *know* or *known*?

What kept Pharaoh from knowing God?

What keeps us from knowing God?

What helps us know God?

How does knowing God make a difference in your life?

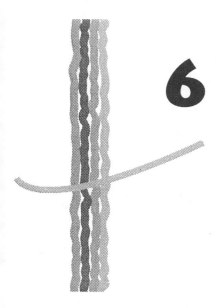

6

DELIVERANCE: PASSOVER AND THE LAST SUPPER

Background from the Author

Some participants will find the death of every first-born in Egypt to be a disturbing idea, leading to questions about why every family should suffer for the sins of the Pharaoh. I have introduced the session by showing how the tenth plague is connected with the Pharaoh's efforts at genocide in Exodus 1. The idea is, let the punishment fit the crime. As for the ordinary people in Egypt, it is true of every nation: Ordinary people do suffer for the sins of their rulers. But questions of this kind can be discussed without end, so let us try not to take too much time away from the main theme, which is the relationship between Passover and the Lord's Supper.

One detail may raise a question, the month-name Abib in Exodus 13:4. There were several changes in the calendar during the Old Testament period. Abib is one of four old Canaanite month-names that are preserved. The others are Ziv (1 Kings 6:1), Ethanim (1 Kings 8:2), and Bul (1 Kings 6:38). Sometimes the months were simply numbered, as in Exodus 12:2. Eventually, the Babylonian month-names were adopted, and they are used to this day. So, the month called Abib in the early period, and later called the first month, is now called Nisan (as in Nehemiah 2:1).

Jeremiah's promise of the New Covenant is mentioned only in this session, and the group may wonder why no more is said about it. The reason is that the Lord's Supper will become a natural part of two more sessions: number 8, in connection with the gift of the manna, and number 9, in connection with the Sinai covenant. This is just the first install-ment in the discussion of the sacrament. It may be useful for you to look ahead, in order to see what aspects of the discussion should be postponed for later, if possible.

The difference in date between John and the Synoptic Gospels may be troublesome to some participants, but there is no way I know to resolve the difficulty. The fact that the day began at sunset sometimes complicates matters for us, so the following chart may be helpful:

	Thursday Last Supper	Friday Crucifixion	Saturday
Synoptics	13th and eve of 14th—Passover Meal	14th—Passover and eve of 15th	
John	12th and eve of 13th	13th and eve of 14th—Passover Meal	14th—Passover and eve of 15th

All agree that Jesus died on Friday and was raised on Sunday, but do not agree on what days of the month these two events occurred. For John, Jesus died on the afternoon before Passover, when the lambs were being sacrificed. For the Synoptics, he died on the afternoon of Passover. It seems likely that historical accuracy was less important to John than it is to us. Since everyone agreed that Jesus' death occurred at Passover time, John thought it valuable to associate it with the sacrifice of the lamb.

This is one of the parts of Exodus that I did not use in *Theology in Exodus*, so other com-mentaries are likely to prove useful. If you can obtain a copy of the Passover Seder it may be of interest to some members of the group. Discussion of the aspects of memory and hope that appear in the Communion service will be facilitated if you have copies of sev-eral different worship books to consult, since the service has been changed over the years, and it varies from one denomination to another.

SESSION PLANS

Learning Objectives

This session is intended to enable participants to:

1. Discuss the importance of ritual.

2. Retell the Exodus story by participating in a Passover ritual.

3. Identify several Jewish roots of our Christian Communion Service.

Resources You May Need

Bibles, chalkboard or newsprint

Food and materials for Seder Meal including tablecloths, candles and matches, communion chalice or large goblet, cushions, paper plates, cups, napkins, bowls, salt, pitchers of juice to represent wine, matzo, horseradish, parsley or celery, haroset (chopped apples, nuts, cinnamon, and red wine) communion liturgies

Copies of "A Passover Haggadah," "Seder Readings," and the worksheet "A Personal Eucharistic Prayer"

Leadership Strategy

SETTING THE STAGE

1. **Prayer from the Psalms.** Read Psalm 66:1-12. If you want the group to read the Psalm together, photocopy it from "Prayers from the Psalms" in the Appendix.

and/or

Opening Prayer. Offer your own prayer of thanksgiving for God's saving power.

2. **Discussing the Importance of Ritual.** Invite the group to think about how we ritualize significant events in our lives and history. Examples might include family celebrations such as wedding anniversaries, national observances such

as Armistice Day, and local community remembrances such as a founder's day or remembering a flood. Ask, "How do rituals of remembrance shape our identities and our understanding of history? How do they influence or shape the future?" (10 minutes)

EXPLORING THE SCRIPTURE

1. **Introducing the Theme.** Remind the group that Chapters 12 and 13 represent an intermingling of historical narrative and ritual observance. They contain an account of the tenth plague, the death of all the Egyptian first-born, instructions for the ritual observance of Passover, laws concerning the first-born, and the start of the exodus from Egypt. (If you wish to cite scripture references for each topic, refer to the section "The Climax" in the *Resource Book*.) From its early beginnings, this story was remembered as it was reenacted through liturgical worship. (3 minutes)

and/or

Researching the Ritual of First Fruits. Invite the group to look up Deuteronomy 26:1-11 and have a volunteer read the passage aloud. Ask:

- What action is called for?

- Why is this to be done?

- What kind of attitude toward life does this ritual instill?

- What parallel rituals or customs from other cultures or faith traditions can you think of?

or

Responding to the *Resource Book*. Read Exodus 4:22-23 and 13:11-16. Read or summarize Dr. Gowan's explanation, found on pages 52-53 of the *Resource Book*, of the sacrifice of first-born males and the offering of all "first fruits" to God as:

- An act of gratitude

- Acknowledging the sovereignty of God over everything

- Reversal of the 10th plague

- Remembrance of Israel's deliverance

- Acknowledging the cost of that deliverance

- Israel as God's "first born."

How does acting out such beliefs affect personal and corporate faith? (10 minutes)

2. **A Seder Meal.** Because the Exodus story was preserved through liturgy and ritual, it is fitting to enter the story through its liturgy, the Seder meal, using "A Passover Haggadah," and the "Seder Readings" which you will find at the end of this chapter. How the group celebrates this meal will depend upon the time and place of your meeting. Here are four possibilities: (1) incorporate the Seder meal liturgy into a luncheon or supper meeting, either "brown bag" or "potluck" (25-40 minutes); (2) follow the liturgy only, eating the symbolic foods described in the service (15-20 minutes); (3) enact the ritual using imaginary food and props if constraints of time and space prevent the use of real food (10-15 minutes); or (4) invite a Jewish friend or rabbi to talk about or conduct the service for the group, adding additional commentary and personal experiences and interpretations (60-75 minutes). If a rabbi is going to conduct a service, be sure to show him or her the liturgy you are planning to use. Your guest may want to provide the Haggadah instead of using this script. It is important that your guest feel comfortable in a Christian setting and that the group respect the Jewish traditions and beliefs being represented and shared.

To set up for the Seder Meal, use one long table or several tables. If possible, use paper or linen table covering and candles. Near the leader's place, set a "cup for Elijah" (communion chalice or other large goblet). Also at the head of the table place the Seder plate containing the following items: a roasted bone, (traditionally a lamb shank, but any meat bone, even a chicken neck may be used), a roasted egg (hard-boiled then roasted at 400 degrees for 30 minutes), bitter herbs (horseradish), haroset (a mixture of chopped apples, nuts, cinnamon, and red wine), and a green vegetable (usually parsley or celery).

Put cushions on some of the chairs, or at least on the leader's chair. Designate a host or hostess for each 8-10 people to serve food and refill "wine" glasses. Place small paper plates, glasses, napkins, and pitchers of "wine" on the tables. Set out plates of matzos for each 8-10 people, each plate containing three whole matzos. Place bowls of salt water within easy reach of every guest. Set out bowls of water for ritual hand-washing and designate persons to carry these bowls to each guest at the appropriate points in the service. As the liturgy begins, serve the following to each person: bitter herbs (horseradish), green vegetable (parsley or celery), haroset (made by combining chopped apples, nuts, cinnamon, and red wine).

Ahead of time, assign "The Four Questions" to one or more volunteers. To tell the "Story of Oppression and Liberation," assign four good readers the "Seder Readings" which you will find following the Seder Haggadah, or ask 3-4 volunteers to tell parts of the Exodus story in their own words.

and

Reflect on the Experience. After the Seder service, invite group members to reflect on the experience. Ask, "What was familiar? What was new? What insights and feelings did the service invoke?" (10-20 minutes)

3. **Connecting Passover and Communion.** Read aloud Luke 22:1-20 and 1 Corinthians 11:23-26. Ask:

   - Which elements or themes are most meaningful to you?

   - Which, if any, are problematic for you?

   - What connections in language, theme, and elements do you see between the Seder service and the description of the Last Supper in these passages? (e.g. prayer over the cup; breaking the bread; the command for future generations to carry on the ritual; the call to remember; blood as a symbol for deliverance; a reference to future fulfillment).

   - How does understanding the Passover Seder enrich your appreciation of the Christian Communion Service? (20 minutes)

or

Reflecting on Your Communion Service. Divide into groups of 3-4 and give each group a copy of one or more Communion liturgies used by your congregation. If a service of Communion is not printed in your hymnal or prayer book, ask your minister for a copy. Have the group read through the service, making a list of the elements it has in common with the Seder service (for example, hymns of praise, retelling the original story). Invite the small groups to discuss how being familiar with the Passover Seder adds to their understanding of the Communion Service. After 15-20 minutes, bring the whole group together and compare the lists they have made. Add any of the following elements that may not have been included:

Hymns of praise

Remembering - retelling the original story

Bread

Wine

Pouring out of blood

Prayers recalling great acts of God and ancestors of the faith

Quotations from the original institution ("It shall be as a memorial," "Do this in remembrance")

Theme of sacrifice (the lamb, Jesus as the Lamb of God)

Breaking the bread

Eating and drinking together

Bringing the past into the present by re-enactment

Future coming anticipated (Elijah, Jesus' return)

Prayers of thanksgiving

Invite the participants' observations and questions. Conclude the discussion by highlighting the role of corporate memory in the rituals of Passover and Communion as discussed in the *Resource Book* under the headings The Last Supper and Memory and Hope. The discussion might bring out the following points:

- The present community is identified and strengthened through the shared story.

- Remembering what God has done in the past gives hope for the future.

- The will and promise of God is to save. (20-25 minutes)

CLOSING

1. **Personal Prayers.** Distribute copies of the worksheet "A Personal Eucharistic Prayer," and give group members a few minutes to complete the prayer. Invite those who are willing to do so to read their prayers. After each person's prayer, the group may respond with the refrain printed in bold at the bottom of the worksheet. (10 minutes)

and/or

Corporate Prayer. Read a prayer of thanksgiving from the Communion or Seder liturgy used earlier. (2 minutes)

and/or

A Hymn. Sing together the hymn, "Guide Me, O Thou Great Jehovah." (3 minutes)

Looking Ahead

If you plan to show a segment of the video, *The Ten Commandments*, at the next session (Exploring 1), preview the video and set the tape at the point where you want to begin. Check to be sure the video equipment is working properly and that you or a designated volunteer knows how to operate it.

Another option for the next session (Exploring 1) suggests assigning 4 volunteers to tell parts of the biblical story, each from the point of view of a particular character. If you choose this option, make the suggested assignments at this session.

The next session also suggests looking at your congregation's service of baptism (Exploring 3; Closing). You may find this service in your hymnal or prayer book.

Or ask your minister for a copy. If you decide to use water in a ritual of remembering baptism (Closing 1), ask your minister if you may use the congregation's baptismal bowl, or locate another suitable bowl.

A Seder Haggadah

"Haggadah" means "to tell." "Seder" means "order." The purpose of the *order* of the *Seder* is to *tell* the story of the Passover and the Exodus. On the Seder table is the Seder Plate containing a *roasted bone* to remind us of the sacrificial lamb offered in the Jerusalem Temple, a *roasted egg* to remind us of festival offerings in the temple, *bitter herbs* to remind us of the bitterness of slavery in Egypt, *haroset* to remind us of the clay and mortar used by the Israelites when they made bricks for Pharaoh, and a *green vegetable* to remind us of springtime, the season of Passover, when nature blossoms into new life. Also on the Seder table is a special cup reserved for the Prophet Elijah.

FESTIVAL CANDLE LIGHTING

After a welcome by the leader, the candles are lighted.

All: **Blessed are you, O Lord our God, King of the Universe, who has sanctified us with your commandments and commanded us to kindle the festival lights.**

I. PRAYER OF SANCTIFICATION AND THE FIRST CUP (*Cups are filled.*)

Leader: Blessed are you, O Lord our God, King of the Universe, creator of the fruit of the vine.

All: **Praised are you, Lord our God, King of the Universe, who has chosen us, sanctified us with your teachings, and given us this day to celebrate our freedom in remembrance of Israel's going out from Egypt. Blessed are you, O Lord our God, who sanctifies Israel and the festival seasons.** (*All raise cups and drink.*)

II. HANDWASHING

We always wash hands before we eat and we recite a special benediction, but since we are not yet ready to eat, we do not say the benediction at this point.

III. EATING A GREEN VEGETABLE

Leader: The green vegetable on your plate represents spring and the rebirth of hope. We dip the vegetable in salt water to remind us of the tears our Hebrew ancestors shed when they were slaves. (*All dip the celery or parsley into a bowl of salt water and eat.*)

All: **Blessed are you, O Lord our God, King of the Universe, who creates the fruit of the earth.**

IV. THE BREAD OF AFFLICTION: BREAKING THE MATZO

The leader—or the leader of each table—breaks the middle matzo in two pieces and leaves one piece in the matzo cloth or tray. The other piece becomes the Afikoman, which the leader wraps in a napkin and sets aside. Children are allowed to try to take the Afikoman and hide it, and to receive a reward before returning it. At the end of the meal, the Afikoman will be broken and each guest will receive a piece.

V. TELLING THE STORY OF THE EXODUS AND THE SECOND CUP

Leader: (*Lifts the matzo and the Seder Plate*). This is the bread of affliction which Israel ate in the land of Egypt.

All: **It is also a symbol of the pain the Jewish people have suffered over the centuries and the oppression many people still endure in the world today. It represents our hope that next year humankind will be free from all oppression.**

Four Questions (traditionally asked by the youngest child)

1. Why is this night different from all other nights? On all other nights, we eat either leavened or unleavened bread. Why on this night do we eat only matzo?

2. On other nights we eat any herb we wish. Why on this night do we eat only bitter herbs?

3. On all other nights we do not dip herbs even once. Why on this night do we dip twice?

4. On all other nights we eat either in a sitting or reclining position. Why on this night do we recline?

Leader: This night is different from all other nights because on this night we tell the story of one of the great events of our history. As we celebrate the meal, listen for the answers to the four questions. At this point, I will answer only the last question, "Why do we recline?" When we were slaves in Egypt, we had to eat in a hurry, often standing or squatting on the ground. Today we are no longer slaves! We recline on cushions to celebrate our freedom and our trust in God who frees us from all oppression!

The Story of Oppression and Liberation: Readings or Impromptu Story-Telling

Recalling the Ten Plagues: blood, frogs, lice, flies, cattle disease, boils, hail, locusts, darkness, slaying of the first-born. (*Wine is poured into any empty cups. As each plague is mentioned, the participants spill out a drop of wine into their plates (or dip a finger into the wine and then touch the plate). According to ancient Jewish tradition, this is done to temper joy by expressing compassion for the suffering of the Egyptians.*)

Leader: In every generation it is our duty to regard ourselves as if we personally had come forth out of Egypt. As we drink the second cup, we remember that it was not only our ancestors that God redeemed, but ourselves as well.

The Second Cup (*Cups are refilled and raised.*)

All: **Blessed are you, O Lord our God, King of the Universe, who redeemed us and who redeemed our ancestors from Egypt. God of our fathers and mothers, bring us to other festivals and holy days in peace, happy in the building of your city and joyous in your service.** (*All drink.*)

VI. HAND WASHING

Leader: We are now ready to enjoy the Seder meal. Before we eat, we wash our hands and say a blessing.

All: **Blessed are you, O Lord our God, King of the Universe, who has sanctified us with your commandments and commanded us concerning the washing of the hands.**

VII. BLESSING

Leader: The unleavened bread reminds us that, in the haste of their departure from Egypt, our ancestors had to take along unleavened dough. (*The leader raises the matzo.*)

All: **Blessed are you, Lord our God, Ruler of the Universe, who brings forth bread from the earth. Blessed are you, Lord our God, who sanctified us with your teachings and commanded us to eat of matzo.**

VIII. EATING THE MATZO

The leader breaks the top matzo and distributes a piece to each guest. All eat matzo.

IX. THE BITTER HERB

Leader: The bitter herbs remind us of the bitterness that the Egyptians caused our ancestors. As we read in Exodus: "They made their lives bitter with hard labor in mortar and bricks and in all manner of field labor." The bitter herbs also remind us of the heroic spirit of the people of Israel who, instead of becoming embittered by their suffering, were sustained and strengthened. As earlier we dipped our green vegetable in salt water, we now take the bitter herbs and dip them into the Haroset, for on this night we dip herbs twice. (*All dip.*)

All: Blessed are you, Lord our God, King of the Universe, who made us holy with your teachings and commanded us to eat of bitter herbs. (*All eat the bitter herbs.*)

X. THE BITTER HERB AND THE MATZO TOGETHER

The bottom matzo is broken, and each participant takes two pieces, placing some bitter herbs between them to form a "sandwich."

Leader: Now we repeat the practice of the great Rabbi Hillel, who lived at the time of the Second Temple in Jerusalem. He would eat matzo and bitter herbs together with the Passover lamb in order to fulfill literally the Torah's command: "They shall eat the Paschal lamb together with matzo and bitter herbs. (*All eat the "Hillel Sandwich."*)

XI. THE SEDER MEAL

XII. THE AFIKOMAN

The leader now tries to find the Afikoman. If it cannot be found, the child who has taken and hidden the Afikoman may request a reward (perhaps candy) before returning it. The leader then divides the Afikoman among all the guests and invites them to eat.

XIII. GRACE AFTER THE MEAL AND THE THIRD CUP (*Cups are refilled.*)

Leader: The Torah tells us that after we have eaten and are satisfied, we shall thank God. Therefore, let us join together in a prayer of thanksgiving and in the blessing over the wine.

All: **Blessed are you, O Lord our God, King of the Universe, who sustains us all. We thank you for giving our ancestors a good and broad land as a heritage, for taking us out of bondage in Egypt, for your covenant which you sealed in our flesh, for your Torah which you have taught us, and for the life, grace, and kindness you have bestowed on us.**

All: **Blessed are you, Lord our God, King of the Universe, creator of the fruit of the vine.** (*All raise cups and drink.*)

The Cup of Elijah

(*Wine is poured into the Cup of Elijah.*)

Leader: We pour this cup for a special guest, the Prophet Elijah. According to tradition, Elijah will return one day as a messenger of final deliverance from all forms of oppression. We open the door in expectation. (*The door is opened.*)

All: **Blessed is he who comes in the name of the Lord!** (*The door is closed.*)

XIV. PSALMS OF PRAISE AND THE FOURTH CUP (*Cups are refilled.*)

Leader: When Israel came forth from Egypt, the house of Jacob from a people of alien tongue, Judah became his sanctuary, Israel his domain.

All: **The sea beheld and fled: Jordan turned back.**
The mountains skipped like rams, the hills like the lambs of the flock.

Leader: Why is it, O sea, that you flee? O Jordan, that you turn back?
You mountains, that you skip like rams? You hills, like the lambs of the flock?

All: **Dance, O earth, at the presence of the Lord, at the presence of the God of Jacob. Who turned the rock into pools of water, the flint into flowing springs.** (Psalm 114) (*All lift cups.*) **Blessed are you, Lord our God, Ruler of the Universe, creator of the fruit of the vine.** (*All drink.*)

XV. PRAYER FOR ACCEPTANCE OF OUR SEDER

Leader: As we have been privileged to participate in this Seder meal, we pray that this celebration may be accepted and that we may celebrate it again together next year in freedom and in peace. May all our homeless brothers and sisters who yearn to be in Jerusalem have their wishes fulfilled.

All: **Next year in Jerusalem!**

[Note: This Seder Haggadah uses the 15 elements that are common to the Seder celebration. Books that have been helpful in preparing this resource are *Keeping*

Passover: Everything You Need to Know to Bring the Ancient Tradition to Life and to Create Your Own Passover Celebration by Ira Steingroot (New York: Harper Collins, 1995); *From Ashes to Fire: Services of Worship for the Seasons of Lent and Easter* (Nashville: Abingdon Press, 1979) pp. 214-230; and *The New Model Seder*, edited by Rabbi Sidney Greenberg and S. Allan Sugarman (The Prayer Book Press of Media Judaica, Inc., 1363 Fairfield Ave., Bridgeport, CN 06605).]

Seder Readings

Reader 1: The book of Deuteronomy states: "My father was a wandering Aramean, and he went down to Egypt and sojourned there; he became a great and important community. The Egyptians dealt harshly with us and oppressed us; they imposed heavy labor upon us." Deuteronomy 26:5-6

Reader 2: The Book of Exodus confirms this story. It tells us that after Joseph died, a new Pharaoh arose who forgot what Joseph and his people had meant for Egypt. This Pharaoh enslaved all Israel and condemned all newborn males to death.

Reader 3: A child named Moses, a descendant of Levi, was saved by Pharaoh's daughter and reared in the palace. Later in life he realized that he was a son of Israel and escaped to the desert. There in Horeb, God revealed himself at the burning bush.

Reader 4: God said: "I am the God of your ancestors, the God of Abraham, the God of Isaac, the God of Jacob. I have indeed seen the misery of my people in Egypt. I have heard their outcry against their slave masters. I have taken heed of their suffering and have come to rescue them from the power of Egypt, and to bring them out of that country into a fine, broad land; it is a land flowing with milk and honey. The outcry of the Israelites has now reached me; yes, I have seen the brutality of the Egyptians toward them. Come now; I will send you to Pharaoh and you shall bring my people Israel out of Egypt." Exodus 3:6-10

Personal Eucharistic Prayer

O GOD, MY _____ (a personal name you wish to use for God),

WHEN I REMEMBER (a time of struggle or hardship you have experienced)

_____

_____.

I GIVE THANKS THAT (how you now see God's help and deliverance at that time)

_____

_____.

I OFFER YOU NOW (something you wish to dedicate or give or promise to God)

_____

_____.

AND I TRUST THAT (a future hope or expectation you have)_____

_____

_____.

Group Response: **"Remember the day on which you came out of Egypt, out of the
house of slavery, because the Lord brought you out from there by
strength of hand."** (13:3)

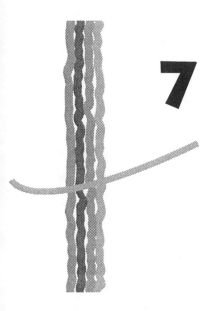

7 FINAL VICTORY: THE WONDER AT THE SEA

Background from the Author

A classroom-size map of the Nile delta region and the Sinai peninsula will be most helpful for this session and the next. If one is not available, at least one Bible atlas should be accessible for the group, since the map will make it obvious that the crossing did not take place at the Red Sea.

Curiosity about how the crossing occurred may take up class time. Some participants may have heard of the theory that the volcanic eruption that destroyed most of the island of Thera (Santorini) in the Aegean region (c. 1450 B.C.), could have created a recession of the sea followed by a tidal wave. This is probably not the answer, for it doesn't fit the date of c. 1250 for the exodus, and it would require the Hebrews to be taking the coast road, which Exodus 13:17 explicitly says they did not do.

Some may be surprised to find references to sea monsters in the poetry of the Old Testament. Isaiah 51:9 speaks of Rahab and the dragon, and in my comment I also mentioned Leviathan. These are echoes of the mythology associated with creation that was prevalent throughout the ancient Near East. Obviously, Israelites were familiar with those ideas. These myths spoke of the victory of the creator god over the forces of chaos as a battle between the god and a sea monster. Those myths themselves do not appear in the Old Testament, since they contained references to more than one god, and that was rejected by the Old Testament authors. But when Yahweh was praised for his victory over the

Sea, poets sometimes could not resist using the old theme of victory over a sea monster. This is the extravagant language of poetry, and we should understand it as metaphor, not as teaching that chaos monsters really exist. The Hebrew word *tannin* (usually translated "dragon") is used in Job 7:12; Psalm 74:13; Isaiah 27:1 and 51:9. Rahab (no relationship to the woman of Jericho by that name) is used in Job 26:12 and Psalm 89:10. Leviathan appears in Job 41:1; Psalm 74:14 and Isaiah 27:1. The influence of Yahwistic theology appears in an interesting way with reference to these characters, for they get "de-mythologized" in some passages where they are no longer enemies of God, but God's "playthings," as one commentator called them. See Psalms 104:26; 148:7; and Genesis 1:21.

We seem to have an instinctive feeling about water as a threat to life that has led to the creation of many sayings: Sink or swim. Getting one's feet wet. Just keeping one's head above water. Engulfed. Up to one's neck. You may think of more. One of the strongest words we have for disaster, "cataclysm," is derived from the Greek word for flood. Once we recognize that instinctive feeling we understand better the use of water imagery in the Psalms as a way of expressing a threat to life of any kind. Psalms 18:16; 32:6; 69:1, 2, 14-15 are examples.

Baptism has been a long-debated subject in Christendom. It is not my intention in this session to introduce every aspect of that, but only to remind participants of the symbolic meaning of the use of water in the sacrament.

SESSION PLANS

Learning Objectives

This session is intended to enable participants to:

1. Tell the story of Israel's journey through the water to freedom.

2. Name some of the challenges and costs of freedom for Israel and for our lives today.

3. Describe some ways that remembering the Wonder at the Sea can offer hope in the midst of current problems.

4. Draw connections between the story of the Wonder at the Sea and the sacrament of baptism.

Resources You May Need

Bibles

Chalkboard or newsprint and markers

The Ten Commandments or *The Prince of Egypt* video

Map showing the route of the Exodus

Copies of a service of baptism used by your congregation

A baptismal bowl or other suitable bowl to use as a reminder of baptism

Copies of worksheets "Moses' Counsel in Times of Trouble," "Memory and Hope," and "The Wonder at the Sea and Christian Baptism"

Leadership Strategy

SETTING THE STAGE

1. **Prayer from the Psalms**. Read Psalm 114. If you want the group to read the Psalm together, photocopy it from "Prayers from the Psalms" in the Appendix. (3 minutes)

and/or

Opening Prayer. Pray in your own words asking to know God as the One who saves. (3 minutes)

2. **Debate: To Follow Moses or Not?** Read aloud Exodus 14:9-12, Israel's complaint that it would have been better to serve the Egyptians than to die in the wilderness. On chalkboard or newsprint, write, "Shall we follow Moses into Freedom? - YES or NO?" Divide into groups of 4-8; then ask each group to subdivide into 2 "debate teams," one to argue "yes," the other "no." For example, if each group gathers at a separate table, one side of the table might be the "yes" team, the other the "no" team. Suggest that spouses separate into different teams. Give the teams about 5 minutes to plan their debating strategy, thinking of as many points as they can to support their side of the debate. Then reconvene the original groups of 4-8, and hold a debate between its "yes" and "no" teams. (10-15 minutes)

Discussion: Costs of Freedom. Read aloud Exodus 14:9-12. Lead a discussion with the whole group about the challenges and costs of freedom. Ask, "What would be the benefits of returning to slavery? Of going forward into freedom? What kinds of things can hold us as 'prisoners' or 'slaves'"? List their answers on chalkboard or newsprint. Ask the participants to reflect quietly for a few minutes about circumstances in their own lives that hold them as slaves or prisoners. Then ask, "What are the challenges or costs of freedom?" List their answers in short words or phrases on chalkboard or newsprint. Encourage them to compare the two sets of lists. (10 minutes)

EXPLORING THE SCRIPTURE

1. **Video.** Show a short segment from the movie, *The Ten Commandments* or *The Prince of Egypt*, showing the incident of the crossing of the sea. (Perhaps a class member will have the video, or rent it from a video store.) Ask, "How is the movie version of the crossing of the Red Sea different from the way the *Resource Book* suggests that it probably happened?" The discussion should bring out the following points:

   • Tracing the route of the Exodus on a map makes it obvious that the Israelites did not cross the Red Sea.

   • The words translated "Red Sea" are "Reed Sea" in the original Hebrew.

   • We cannot be certain of the historical details of this event.

   Ask volunteers to read aloud Joshua 24:6-7 and Nehemiah 9:9-11. Then read aloud the following statement from the *Resource Book*:

   We can never know exactly what happened. It is not important. What is important is Israel's recollection that when threatened with death by water or by sword they were delivered, and from that point on they were truly free from Egypt.

   Ask, "Do you agree with this statement? Why or why not? What was most important about the way Israel remembered this event?" (15-20 minutes)

and/or

Discussion: The Wonder at the Sea. Read aloud Exodus 14:5-9. Ask:

- What were some of the feelings the Hebrew people might have had as they were trapped between the waters and the pursuing Egyptian army?

- How might they have felt when God led them safely through the waters? (10 minutes)

or

First-Person Accounts of the Event. Ahead of time, ask four volunteers to prepare to tell in their own words the part of the story that is told in the following verses from Exodus. Suggest that they pretend to be Moses or one of the Israelites, using "I" and "we." Have a map available for their use.

(1) 14:1-4 Pretend to be Moses

(2) 14:5-9 Pretend to be an Israelite

(3) 14:10-14 Pretend to be an Israelite

(4) 14:15-29 Pretend to be Moses (10 minutes)

2. **Responding to Moses' Counsel.** Read aloud Exodus 14:10-15, Moses' speech to the people of Israel when they were caught between the sea and Pharaoh's army. Distribute the Worksheet A, "Moses' Counsel in Times of Crisis." Invite the participants to reflect quietly and to do the worksheet. After 8-10 minutes, invite them to talk with a partner, someone other than a spouse, about their reflections. (15 minutes)

or

Small-Group Reflection: Memory and Hope. In the section, "Water as a Threat: God's Victory over 'the Waters,'" the *Resource Book* names some times when remembering God's victory over the waters of the Red Sea gave the people of Israel hope to face a new crisis. Invite volunteers to read aloud the following passages, briefly outlining the circumstances in which each was spoken:

- Joshua 24:6-7 (part of Joshua's plea to the loosely-organized tribes of Israel to put aside foreign gods and to unite in serving Yahweh).

- Isaiah 43:16-19 (spoken by the prophet to the exiles in Babylon).

- Nehemiah 9:9-11 (spoken by the prophet Ezra, urging the returning exiles to rebuild their temple and their lives).

- Acts 7:36 (spoken by Stephen to those who persecuted him for following Christ).

Then in groups of 4-6, do Worksheet B, "Memory and Hope." After 20-25 minutes, bring the whole group together and have a spokesperson from each group read the Psalm, prayer, or paragraph the group wrote. (25-30 minutes)

3. **Drawing Connections with Baptism.** In the *Resource Book* section "The Two-Fold Use of Water in the New Testament," Dr. Gowan notes that in 1 Corinthians Paul makes passing through the sea a parallel to baptism. In Romans, Paul associates the threatening aspects of water with baptism, so that baptism becomes a symbolic death. In 1 Peter, Peter draws a parallel between the waters of the great flood and baptism and emphasizes water's function as a cleansing agent. Invite volunteers to read aloud 1 Corinthians 10:1-2, Romans 6:3-4, and 1 Peter 3:20-22. Then in small groups, complete and discuss Worksheet C, "The Wonder at the Sea and Christian Baptism." After 15-20 minutes, have a volunteer from each group report briefly on the group's discussion. To save time and avoid repetition, ask the reporter from one group to summarize the group's answers to question 1, inviting other groups to add additional points. Ask the reporter from a different group to summarize the group's answers to question 2, and so forth. (25-30 minutes)

or

Reflecting on your Service of Baptism. Read aloud selected parts of your congregation's service of baptism, inviting the group to listen for references to the Wonder at the Sea. (Ask your pastor for a copy of the service of baptism if it is not printed in your hymnal or prayer book.) Ask, "What parallels do you see between the Wonder at the Sea and Christian baptism?" The parallels they suggest may include the following:

- In both, God does for us what we cannot do for ourselves.

- Both use water.

- Both involve death of the old and birth of the new.

- Both begin a new relationship with God. (10-15 minutes)

CLOSING

1. **Prayer and Reaffirmation of Baptism**. Close with a prayer from a service for affirmation of baptism used by your congregation, or read the following prayer. You may incorporate a ritual of remembering baptism into the prayer.

   Eternal God, who parted the waters of the Red Sea allowing your people to cross from slavery into freedom, who blessed your son Jesus as he was baptized by John in the waters of the River Jordan, and who sent the disciples forth to baptize all nations by water and the Spirit, thank you for the new life born out of these waters and for continuing to do new things in our lives. Thank you especially for the water of our own baptism through which we have died to sin and are raised to new life in Christ. *(Here you may sprinkle water over the group, using your congregation's baptismal bowl or another appropriate bowl. Or walk through the group, touching each member's forehead with water.)* Remembering our baptism, we rejoice in the gift of water and your Spirit, and we ask you to satisfy our thirsts with living water. Thanks, praise, and glory to you, O God of grace. Amen. (5-10 minutes)

   and/or

   Sentence Prayers. Read the one-sentence prayers the groups wrote in Exploring the Scripture 2 (Worksheet A).

   or

   The Song of Miriam. Read together Exodus 15:1-2. Introduce the reading by observing that the song of celebration in verse 1, repeated in verse 21, is the Song of Miriam, one of the oldest parts of the Old Testament. (3 minutes)

and/or

Prayer. Close with your own prayer celebrating God's saving power. (3 minutes)

Looking Ahead

The next session (Closing) asks the group to reflect on their own life journeys and fill out a worksheet as they prepare for the group meeting. If you wish to use this option, distribute the worksheet "Life's Journey Remembrance" at the close of this session.

Moses' Counsel in Times of Crisis

The people of Israel were running for their lives! The horses and chariots of Pharaoh's army raged at their heels and ahead of them lay the sea. When they looked back on the advancing Egyptians, they cried out to Moses, "It would have been better for us to serve the Egyptians than to die in the wilderness!" Then Moses spoke these words to them (Exodus 14:10-15).

Read the words slowly; then circle **one** *that you believe God may be saying to you* **now**.

Don't be afraid.

Stand firm.

See the deliverance the Lord will accomplish for you.

The Lord will fight for you.

Keep still.

Go forward.

After reflecting on the way this sentence speaks to your life right now, write a one-sentence prayer.

Memory and Hope

Working as a group

list . . . some problems that face your congregation, your family, or our society. (Some examples are division within the congregation, lack of quality family time, economic injustice, environmental concerns.)

choose . . . one issue that particularly concerns the members of your group.

discuss . . . how remembering God's powerful actions in the past, including God's victory over the sea, might offer hope in the midst of the problem you chose.

write . . . a brief psalm, prayer, or paragraph celebrating God's power to act in this situation. Here is an example: *"O God, when we feel discouraged and frightened about global warming, we remember your victory over the sea, and we gain hope that now you will move people to make the sacrifices needed to conquer this problem. Thank you for your power to bring newness in our world. Amen.*

O GOD, WHEN WE FEEL DISCOURAGED AND FRIGHTENED BECAUSE

_____,

WE REMEMBER_____

_____.

AND WE GAIN HOPE THAT_____

_____.

THANK YOU_____. **Amen.**

The Wonder at the Sea and Christian Baptism

Discuss the following questions:

1. How was the journey through the sea a death and a rebirth for the people of Israel?

    What died?

    What was born?

2. How did this event change Israel's relationship with God?

3. What parallels do you see between the Wonder at the Sea and the Christian sacrament of Baptism? In your discussion, you may want to refer to 1 Corinthians 10:1-2, Romans 6:3-4, and 1 Peter 3:20-22.

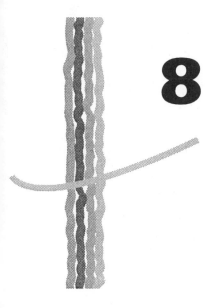

8

WILDERNESS: A NEW AND DANGEROUS LIFE

Background from the Author

Chapter 7 of *Theology in Exodus* will provide supplementary material for Sessions 8 through 11. You can probably find at least one picture of Jebel Musa in a Bible dictionary, but the more illustrations of the Sinai desert you can find, the easier it will be to appreciate the hardships facing people who try to live there.

Depending on the group's interests, the importance of having a regular day of rest in our society, which makes virtually no allowances for such a luxury, may be a useful subject to explore.

The Lord's Supper becomes a major part of this session, because of John's interpretation of the feeding of the five thousand. At least one good commentary on John 6 will probably be a help to the group. Raymond Brown's work in the Anchor Bible Commentary series is recommended. Note that the bread of Communion was originally the unleavened bread of the Passover meal, as we saw in Session 6. Now John associates it with the manna given in the wilderness. Jesus' words at the Last Supper, "This is my body," seem to be taken very literally by John when he speaks of eating Jesus' flesh. He has moved from Passover bread and from manna to the idea of Jesus as bread of life (and water of life, as we found in Session 7). This is the concept that has led to debates in the churches over the "real presence" of Christ in the Sacrament. Does the bread actually become the body of Christ (transubstantiation) as the Roman Catholic Church teaches? Is Christ present "in, with, and under" the bread, as Luther taught? Or is Christ really present, but in spirit, as the Reformed churches teach? This course is not the appropriate place to get into that old debate, but I mention it here in order to alert leaders that in some groups John's language may bring it up.

Mekilta is a rabbinic commentary on Exodus, parts of which may have been written as early as the second century A.D. You may find it helpful to look for additional information on the uses of allegory and typology, and the problems associated with them, as you prepare for this session.

SESSION PLANS

Learning Objectives

This session is intended to enable participants to:

1. Tell the story of Israel's wandering in the wilderness in Exodus 15:22-18:27.

2. Relate the Hebrews' experience of being fed manna in the wilderness to their understanding of Jesus as the "Bread of Life."

3. Discuss four ways Christians have interpreted the Old Testament.

4. Apply lessons learned by the Hebrews in the wilderness to their own faith journeys.

Resources You May Need

Bibles, chalkboard or newsprint and markers

Map of the Sinai Peninsula

Copies of the following: Dramatic Reading "Murmuring and Testing in the Wilderness, Worksheet A, "Wilderness Story Pattern," Worksheet B, "We Are Fed by God's Hand," and Worksheet C, "Life Journey Remembrance"

Leadership Strategy

<u>SETTING THE STAGE</u>

1. **Prayer from the Psalms.** Read Psalm 23. If you want the group to read the Psalm together, photocopy it from "Prayers from the Psalms" in the Appendix. (3 minutes)

and/or

Opening Prayer. Offer a prayer inviting God's presence as we study Israel's time in the wilderness. (3 minutes)

2. **Introducing the Theme.** Introduce today's theme as "Wilderness, a new and dangerous life." Note the stark and immediate contrast between the Song of Miriam in 15:21 and the situation presented in 15:22. In the words of Exodus commentator Terence E. Fretheim, "Instead of a land of milk and honey, they got a desert." [*Exodus: Interpretation Bible Commentary* (Louisville: John Knox, 1991) p. 171] As the *Resource Book* notes, the memories of this period in Israel's history are varied and they run deep. (3 minutes)

and

Routes of the Exodus. On a map, point out the possible route(s) of the Exodus described by Dr. Gowan. Ask, "How important is it to know the physical location of Mt. Sinai and the wilderness events? Why?" (5 minutes)

and

Review. Ask:

- Who are the people that are now following Moses?

- Where have they come from?

- How prepared are they for this journey?

- What do you think their expectations were at the end of 15:21? (3-5 minutes)

EXPLORING THE SCRIPTURE

1. **Writing "News."** Using the script, "Murmuring and Testing in the Wilderness," located at the end of this chapter, assign volunteers to read the parts of *the Lord, Moses*, and a *narrator*. Invite everyone else to participate as "the people," ad-libbing their responses. After the dramatic reading, divide into groups of 3-4. Have each group write a UPI wire report from "on the scene with Moses and the Hebrew People" including quotations from key figures. Appoint one person in each group to act as anchor person on the evening news with other members of the group providing live interviews with "on the scene" reporters. Present the "reports" in the large group. (25-30 minutes)

or

Research: Wilderness Story Pattern. In groups of 3-4, complete Worksheet A "Wilderness Story Pattern." Assign one scripture reference to each group, and ask them to fill out the corresponding column. If your group is smaller than 18, omit one or more of the Exodus passages. Note that not every passage will follow the pattern perfectly.

Return to the large group, and have each small group report on its findings. Observe the differences in the way the Lord responds in the Numbers passage. (15 minutes)

and/or

Preparing Report Cards. Divide into four groups. Invite each group to dare to enter the mind of God and to prepare report cards for the Hebrew people based on Exodus 15:22-17:7 and Numbers 11. The groups are to make up their own grading criteria and scales. Make the following assignments:

Group 1. Report Card for the People based on Ex 15:22-17:7

Group 2. Report Card for Moses based on Ex. 15:22-17:7

Group 3. Report Card for the People based on Numbers 11

Group 4. Report Card for Moses based on Numbers 11

Return to the large group and have each group present its report card. Because of the varied recollections from the wilderness period, the report cards will probably differ. Ask:

- How do you account for the different emphases in these accounts?

- Can differing recollections all be valid? Why or why not? (25-30 minutes)

2. **Writing cinquains: We Are Fed by God's Hand.** In groups of 3-4, discuss and complete Worksheet B, "We Are Fed by God's Hand." Then have spokespersons from the groups present their cinquain. (15-20 minutes)

Reflection and Sharing: Jesus as the Bread of Life. Read aloud John 6:1-14, noting that the feeding of the 5000 is the only miracle recorded in all four gospels. Ask, "How did Jesus use the memory of the manna in the wilderness (6:31-32,49,58) to identify himself and his purpose?" Note their responses on chalkboard or newsprint. Then invite participants to talk with another person about what it means for them that "Jesus is the Bread of Life." (10-15 minutes)

and/or

Designing a Church Brochure. Ask the group to read John 6:41-65 silently, noting the parts that are particularly meaningful and any that are troublesome or unclear. Then divide into groups of 3-4. Suggest that the groups take a few minutes to discuss their thoughts about the passage and then design a flier or brochure inviting someone to visit the church, based on these verses. Have them present the brochures in the large group. (20-25 minutes)

3. **Methods of Interpreting the Old Testament.** Dr. Gowan discusses four methods Christians have used to make the Old Testament more "relevant" to Christianity. Referring to the section Israel at War for the First Time in the *Resource Book*, invite participants to name and define each of the four methods. Then discuss the following questions with the whole group:

- What is the appeal of these methods?

- Why might they be inappropriate?

- Can the group think of other Old Testament passages that have been interpreted using one of these methods? (10 minutes)

or

"Interpreting" other Exodus passages. As in 3 above, ask participants to name and define the four methods Christians have used to interpret the Old Testament, referring to the section Israel at War for the First Time in the *Resource Book*. Then divide into groups of 3-4, giving each group one of the passages listed below. Invite the groups to "interpret" their passages using one or more of these methods to "prove" a particular point or cause of their choice. Give the groups permission to exaggerate the possible misuse of these methods to demonstrate their limitations and dangers.

Exodus 15:22-25

Exodus 15:26

Exodus 16:1-8

Exodus 17:1-7

After about 15 minutes, bring the whole group together and invite a representative from each group to share the group's "interpretations." (20-25 minutes)

4. **Writing and Sharing a Sabbath Code.** Read the wilderness Sabbath recollections in 4:22-30 aloud. Then ask:

- What did the Sabbath mean to these people?

- How is Sabbath a gift?

- What does it mean to keep Sabbath today?

- What prevents us from keeping a Sabbath today?

Write the following questions on chalkboard or newsprint, and allow some time for quiet reflection.

- How well do you keep Sabbath?

- How would your life be changed by keeping Sabbath more faithfully?

- Write a Sabbath code for yourself (like a New Year's Resolution).

Invite group members to talk about their Sabbath codes in pairs. (20-25 minutes)

and/or

Discussion: Jethro's Advice. In your own words, briefly relate the account of Moses' meeting with his father-in-law Jethro described in Exodus 18:1-12. Then ask a volunteer to read aloud 18:13-27. Ask:

- What is striking about this passage?

- What can this story teach us about gifts, leadership, and sources of wisdom?

If time allows, invite group members to write diary entries that Moses or Jethro might have made at the end of this visit. Ask some volunteers to read their entries. (15 minutes)

CLOSING

1. **Sharing Life Journeys.** In groups of 3-4, invite participants to tell some of the memories that they wrote on the worksheet, "Life Journey Remembrance," which they filled out as they prepared for this session. (You will have given the worksheet to them at the end of the previous session.) Encourage the small groups to listen to each speaker without interruption. After about 15 minutes, bring the whole group together. Invite those who wish to do so to read the sentence prayers they wrote on the worksheet. Close by having the whole group read God's Promise for the Journey given at the end of the worksheet. (20 minutes)

and/or

Closing Prayer. Close with your own prayer expressing thanks both for God's care on our life journeys and for the growth we experience through life's challenges. (3 minutes)

Looking Ahead

One option for the next session suggests playing a CD or audiocassette of thunderstorm effects (Setting the Stage). You might ask at this session if anyone has such a CD or audiocassette. If not, most record stores will have one.

The next session (Exploring 3) also suggests reenacting the covenant-sealing ceremony. This activity can be very effective and also simple to plan. Look ahead to this option now. You will need to designate an area where people may stand or sit in a circle and to locate something to use as an altar. Your sanctuary is a possibility if it will be available and has movable chairs. Or perhaps an altar used in a children's worship might serve. If not, a small table or even several chairs could suffice. The activity suggests using a stuffed animal (from the nursery or a family with young children) as the "sacrificial animal." And you will need a bowl to hold "sacrificial blood" (water).

Murmuring
and Testing in the Wilderness

Exodus 15:22 - 17:7

Narrator: After Israel crossed the Red Sea, Moses led them into the Desert of Shur. They traveled for three days without finding water. On the fourth day they found water, but it was too bitter to drink. They named the place Marah, meaning "bitter." *The people grumbled against Moses! (Pause for grumbling.)*

Then Moses cried out to Yahweh.

Moses: Help us!

Yahweh: **Here, I'm going to throw this piece of wood in the water. Now taste the water!**

Narrator: Moses tasted it and it was sweet! Then Yahweh made a law for them, and tested them.

Yahweh: **I am Yahweh your God, and I cure your diseases. If you obey me by following my laws and teachings, I won't punish you with the diseases I sent on the Egyptians.**

Narrator: Later the Israelites wandered through the western edge of the Sinai Desert in the direction of Mount Sinai. *There they started complaining to Moses and Aaron! (Pause.)* Then Yahweh said to Moses:

Yahweh: **I will send bread down from heaven like rain. Each day the people can go out and gather only enough for that day. But on the sixth day of each week they must gather and cook twice as much.**

Narrator: After awhile, *the people* looked out toward the desert and saw the bright glory of Yahweh in a cloud. *And they exclaimed in amazement! (Pause.)*

That evening, a lot of quail came and landed everywhere in the camp, and the next morning dew covered the ground. After the dew had gone, the desert was covered with thin flakes that looked like frost. The people had never seen anything like this, and *they started asking each other questions about it! (Pause for murmured questions.)* Moses answered.

Moses: This is the bread that the LORD has given you to eat. And he commands you to gather enough for your family and not to keep any overnight.

Narrator: Some of them disobeyed, but the next morning what they kept was stinking and full of worms. Each morning, they gathered as much as they needed. However, on the sixth day of the week, everyone gathered enough for two days, for Yahweh had said:

Yahweh: **Tomorrow is the Sabbath, a sacred day of rest to honor me. So gather all you want to bake or boil, and make sure you save enough for tomorrow.**

Narrator: So the people obeyed, and the next morning the food smelled fine and had no worms. Once, while they were camped at a place called Rephidim, *the people complained to Moses because there was no water for them to drink. (Pause for complaining.)*

Then Moses prayed to Yahweh,

Moses: What am I going to do with these people? They are about to stone me to death!

Yahweh: **Take some of the leaders with you and go ahead of the people. Take along your walking stick that you used to strike the Nile River, and when you get to the rock at Mt. Sinai, strike the rock with the stick and pure water will pour out.**

Narrator: Moses did this while the people watched. *And the people exclaimed in amazement! (Pause.)* Moses named the place Massah, which means "testing" and Meribah, which means "complaining."

Wilderness Story Pattern

What Happens	Exodus 14:1-31	Exodus 15:22-26	Exodus 15:27-16:30	Exodus 17:1-7	Numbers 20:1-13
A note concerning movement					
Description of the problem					
People complain					
Moses cries to the Lord					
The Lord responds					
Moses obeys					
Results					

We Are Fed by God's Hand
Exodus 16

Discuss:

- How do you think the Israelites felt when they discovered and ate the manna in the wilderness?

- When (if ever) have you felt that you were fed by God's hand?

As a group, write a cinquain, in response to your discussion. A cinquain is a structured 5-line poem. Write one word in each blank below.

_____

(a 1-word name for God)

_____   _____

(2 words describing God)

_____   _____   _____

(3 words suggesting a need or situation)

_____   _____   _____   _____

(4 words describing God's actions or nature)

_____

(a closing word, exclamation or synonym for God)

Life Journey Remembrance

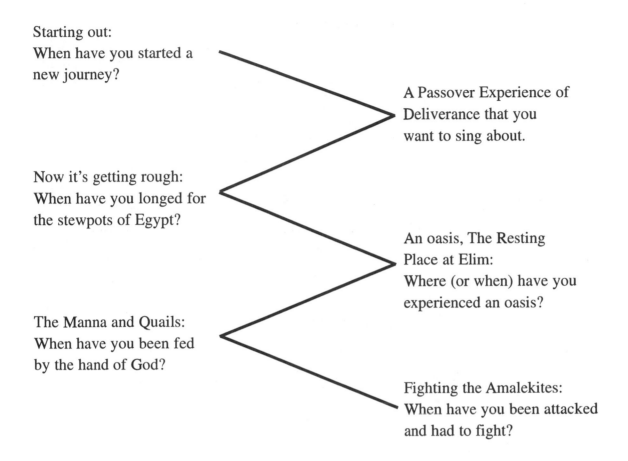

Starting out:
When have you started a
new journey?

A Passover Experience of
Deliverance that you
want to sing about.

Now it's getting rough:
When have you longed for
the stewpots of Egypt?

An oasis, The Resting
Place at Elim:
Where (or when) have you
experienced an oasis?

The Manna and Quails:
When have you been fed
by the hand of God?

Fighting the Amalekites:
When have you been attacked
and had to fight?

GOD'S PROMISE FOR THE JOURNEY:

Do not fear, for I have redeemed you;

I have called you by name, you are mine.

When you pass through the waters I will be with you;

and through the rivers they will not overwhelm you. (Is. 43:1-2)

Write a sentence prayer to share in our closing:_____

9

COVENANT: GOD'S PROMISE TO THE PEOPLE

Background from the Author

Articles on covenant in Bible dictionaries may provide additional information that will be helpful. You may run across the idea of a covenant with Adam in some sources. The reasons for this are puzzling, since the word "covenant" is never used in Genesis 1-5. The word is used of divine covenants only, with the four mentioned in the *Resource Book* plus the promise of a new covenant.

The ideas introduced briefly in the section on theophany, that the presence of God is both daunting and fascinating, are developed at some length in Chapter 2 of *Theology in Exodus*, "The Numinous." Some groups may find them to be of interest.

The concept of the chosen people has been a troublesome one, at times. I have perhaps dealt with it too briefly in the *Resource Book*, having been satisfied there to state the important conclusion: chosenness in scripture is never solely for privilege, but always requires responsibility—indeed heavier responsibility than would be expected of others who have not been given special privileges. Even so, in America the idea of special (spiritual!) privilege may seem offensive, in spite of the fact that people seek privileges all the time. The story of God's way of working with the human race, as told in scripture, however, indicates that God begins with certain individuals, chosen to carry out a special work. That work is addressed to a certain group of people, anticipating that they will understand and become the agents who will carry those truths and that way of life to others. So the concept of being chosen is an important one, but one that should never lead to pride.

The brief summary of five aspects of the covenant relationship at the end of the session may provide a useful way for you to conclude your group's discussion. You will find the five elaborated at considerable length in Chapter 7 of *Theology in Exodus*. Note that although I have included aspects 4 and 5 here, they more properly belong with Session 10, and will be developed there.

SESSION PLANS

Learning Objectives

This session is intended to enable participants to:

1. Define *theophany* and identify phenomena and feelings associated with a theophany.

2. Cite several examples of the divine initiative in establishing a covenant relationship.

3. Name five characteristics of the covenant relationship.

4. Relate the sealing of the Covenant at Sinai to Jesus' institution of a new covenant.

Resources You May Need

Bibles, chalkboard or newsprint and markers

Audiocassette or CD of thunderstorm effects

Supplies for the covenant-sealing ritual including something to represent an altar (perhaps a table)

12 "pillars," (perhaps built from children's blocks or paper cups), a sacrificial animal (perhaps a stuffed toy), and a bowl for water to represent "blood of sacrifice"

Copies of Worksheet A, "Theophany," Worksheet B, "Characteristics of the Covenant Relationship," and "A Covenant Litany"

Leadership Strategy

<u>SETTING THE STAGE</u>

1. **Prayer from the Psalms.** Read Psalm 105:1-6. If you want the group to read the Psalm together, photocopy it from "Prayers from the Psalms" in the Appendix. (3 minutes)

and/or

Opening Prayer. Offer your own prayer giving thanks for God's covenant and asking for God's guidance. (3 minutes)

2. **Introducing the Theme.** Introduce the theme for this session as the Covenant initiated by God. Mention that this session will focus on God's side of the divine promise and the way the covenant was sealed. The next session will emphasize human responsibility.

3. **Reflection: Theophany Experiences.** Distribute Worksheet A, "Theophany." Allow a few minutes for the participants to reflect on the worksheet. Then ask them to talk about their reflections in groups of 2 or 3. (15 minutes)

or

Discussion: The Sinai Theophany. Read aloud the description of the theophany in Exodus 19:16-19. Ask:

• What are some things the people saw and heard during these theophanies?

• What feelings do you think these phenomena inspired?

• What other theophanies (times when God came into the presence of the people) can you think of?

List their answers on newsprint or chalkboard in short words and phrases in two columns titled "WHAT HAPPENED" and "HOW THEY FELT." Conclude the discussion by quoting Dr. Gowan's words from the *Resource Book*: "The near presence of God leaves us blessed, but not comfortable." (10 minutes)

or

Reading Scripture with Sound Effects. Play an audiocassette or CD that has thunderstorm sound effects. (Sound effect tapes and CD's are available in many record stores; a member of your group may have one.) Then ask a good reader to read in a strong voice Exodus 19:16-19. Ask, "How do you think the people felt when all this happened?" (5 minutes)

EXPLORING THE SCRIPTURE

1. **Writing Sentence Prayers of Thanksgiving.** Ask volunteers to read aloud the following passages:

    Genesis 9:8-17 (God's covenant with Noah)

    Genesis 17:1-8 (God's covenant with Abraham)

    Exodus 19:4-6 (God's covenant with Moses and the Israelites)

    2 Samuel 7:8-16 (God's covenant with David)

    Jeremiah 31:31-34 (Promise of a new covenant)

    1 Corinthians 11:23-26 (the New Covenant)

Then write one-sentence prayers of thanksgiving for the covenant God has initiated with us. Depending on the amount of time you wish to devote to this activity, invite each person to write a personal prayer or divide into groups of 4-6 and write the prayers as a group. Tell them to save the prayers they write to use in the closing. (personal prayers, 10 minutes; group prayers, 20 minutes)

or

Discussion: Covenant and Grace. Read aloud Exodus 19:3-6 and 20:1-2. Then read aloud the following statement from the *Resource Book*:

The Old Testament does not teach "works salvation"; i.e. the idea that one can (or must) do enough good deeds and avoid enough sins to *earn* God's approval. Israel's story *began*, not with anything the people did, but with God's saving act—the deliverance from Egypt. Both 19:4-6 and the Ten

Commandments begin that way. The order is important: First God saves them and makes them into a people (19:4); next God promises a special role for them in history and that the relationship will continue if they obey. The belief that we are saved by grace, not by our own efforts, and that our part is to believe and respond in faithfulness is thus not something that first appeared in the New Testament. It is already here in Exodus. (*Resource Book*, page 82.)

Ask:

- Do you agree with this statement? Why or why not?

- How does our belief that right relationship is a result of God's grace affect our actions?

- Why is it difficult for some of us to accept this concept?

- Why is it difficult for some of us to trust God's grace? (15 minutes)

2. **Naming Characteristics of the Covenant Relationship.** Ask, "What are some of the characteristics of the covenant between God and human persons?" As characteristics are suggested, list them on chalkboard or newsprint. Invite the group to suggest examples of each one, drawing on their reading of Exodus and on the previous discussion. Be sure their list includes all the elements given in the section "Summarizing the Meaning of the Covenant Relationship" in the *Resource Book*. Then ask, "How would you respond to a friend who said, "I'm offended by the idea that God chooses favorites"? Or write that question on the chalkboard and invite them to write a response to it in groups of 4-6. During the discussion or after the groups report, refer back to their list of characteristics of the covenant relationship, emphasizing that being a "chosen people" means being chosen both for privilege (knowledge of the true God and access to unique blessings) *and* responsibility (to testify to God's nature through words and actions). (10-15 minutes)

or

Finding Examples of Five Characteristics of Covenant. Working in groups of 4-6, fill out Worksheet B, "Characteristics of the Covenant Relationship." If time is short, you may want to assign a different scripture passage (a different column from the worksheet) to each group. They are to read the assigned passage(s) and write examples of each characteristic in the appropriate column. After 10-20 minutes, bring the group together and have spokespersons from the groups read what they have written. Invite them to note similarities and differences among the covenants. Conclude the discussion with Dr. Gowan's statement that the feature that distinguishes the Sinai covenant from the others is the fact that it defines the character of the people of God by spelling out how they should live (*Resource Book*, page 82.) (20-30 minutes)

3. **Ritual of Sealing the Covenant.** Act out the ritual of covenant-sealing described in Exodus 24. Prepare for the ceremony on the spot by assigning 2-4 people to each of the tasks outlined below. (The "people" may be a larger group, and other groups who finish their tasks should also prepare to be "the people.") Choose a strong leader to play Moses. Make copies of the instructions below and distribute them, or write them on chalkboard or newsprint. Tell the groups to use their imagination and to keep the preparations simple; they will only have 10 minutes to prepare.

Moses. Prepare to lead the ceremony as described in Exodus 24:6-8 (Read the Ten Commandments (Exodus 10:1-17) rather than the whole "Book of the Covenant."

Committees to prepare elements of the ceremony:

- **Setup Committee.** *Clear an area where people may stand or sit in a circle, facing the "altar."*

- **Altar Committee.** Prepare the "altar at the foot of the mountain" (24:4). *This might be a table or altar used in children's worship.*

- **Pillar Committee.** Find something to represent the 12 pillars (24:4). *The pillars need not be tall. They could be built of hymnals, paper cups from the kitchen, or blocks from a Church School room.*

- **Burnt Offering Committee.** Find something to represent a burnt offering (24:5). *This might be a chair and a stuffed toy from the nursery.*

- **Sacrificial Blood Committee.** Prepare a basin for "blood" from the burnt offering (24:6). *Any bowl from the kitchen will suffice to hold water that represents the blood of sacrifice.*

The people (24:7-8). Discuss how you will respond to Moses' words. Prepare to recite your response from memory.

After about 10 minutes, gather the group and act out the ceremony. Then ask:

- How did it feel to act out this ancient ritual?

- How does acting out this ritual add to your understanding of Jesus' words in 1 Corinthians 11:25: "This cup is the new covenant in my blood"? (25-30 minutes)

or

Naming the elements of the covenant-sealing ceremony. Invite the group to read Exodus 24:3-8 silently and then to name, in order if possible, the actions that took place in the ceremony of sealing the Sinai covenant. List these actions on chalkboard or newsprint, leaving space after each one in case you need to insert other actions between the ones you have already written so as to list the actions in the order they occurred. In the last item listed, be sure to include Moses' words, "See the blood of the covenant that the LORD has made with you" (24:8). Then have someone read aloud 1 Corinthians 11:25. Ask, "How does learning about the covenant-sealing ritual at Sinai add to your understanding of Jesus' words 'This cup is the new covenant in my blood'?" Conclude the activity by noting Dr. Gowan's statement, "The new covenant would be sealed with [Jesus'] blood, as the Sinai covenant had been sealed with blood long ago" (*Resource Book*, page 85.) (10 minutes)

CLOSING

1. **A Litany.** Read responsively "A Covenant Litany." As you introduce the litany, mention that Part 1 (boldface type) is entirely taken from Exodus, while Part 2 (plain type) contains related ideas introduced later by the prophet Jeremiah and by Jesus. (3 minutes)

and/or

Sentence Prayers. Close with the personal or group prayers of thanksgiving composed in Exploring 1a. (5 minutes)

and/or

Closing Prayer. Close with your own prayer thanking God for establishing the covenant relationship and asking that God's will may be written on our hearts. (3 minutes)

Looking Ahead

Begin thinking ahead to Session 11, which suggests several ways to help the group experience the tabernacle. One option is to lead "A Tour of the Tabernacle," using the script provided. This tour should not be complicated, but you will need to designate a "tour guide," decide with him or her where the tour will take place, and locate several props. An alternate option suggests asking a volunteer to construct a wood, cardboard, or clay model of the tabernacle.

Theophany

A *Theophany* is a manifestation or appearance of God's presence to humans. Below is a list of some of the many *theophanies* in the Bible. Circle the *one* that you most identify with. (Perhaps you will identify with it because it seems closest to your own experience.)

- The angel of the LORD appeared to Moses in a flame of fire out of a bush; he looked, and the bush was blazing, yet it was not consumed (Exodus 3:2).

- The LORD went in front of them in a pillar of cloud by day, to lead them along the way, and in a pillar of fire by night, to give them light (Exodus 13:21).

- On the morning of the third day (when Moses was on the mountain with God) there was thunder and lightning, as well as a thick cloud on the mountain, and a blast of a trumpet so loud that all the people who were in the camp trembled . . . . Now Mount Sinai was wrapped in smoke, because the LORD had descended upon it in fire; the smoke went up like the smoke of a kiln, while the whole mountain shook violently (Exodus 19:16, 18).

- The earth reeled and rocked; the foundations also of the mountains trembled and quaked, because [the LORD] was angry . . . .The LORD also thundered in the heavens, and the Most High uttered his voice (Psalm 18:7, 13).

- And behold, the LORD passed by, and a great and strong wind rent the mountains, . . . but the LORD was not in the wind; and after the wind an earthquake, but the LORD was not in the earthquake; and after the earthquake a fire, but the LORD was not in the fire; and after the fire a *still small voice* (1 Kings 19:11-12 RSV).

Why did you choose the one you circled?

Describe a time when you felt the near presence of God.

Characteristics of the Covenant Relationship

	Genesis 17:1-8	Exodus 19:4-6	Jeremiah 31:31-34	1 Peter 2:9-10
Divine initiative: God establishes the covenant				
Exclusive relationship: No other gods				
Intimate relationship: God cares for people and draws them close				
Obedience: It is not just a one-way relationship				
Reflecting God's character: People are to become a testimony to the world				

A Covenant Litany

God said to Moses: "You have seen what I did to the Egyptians and how I bore you on eagles' wings and brought you to myself. Now therefore, if you obey my voice and keep my commandments, you shall be my treasured possession out of all people."

The First Letter of Peter described the new covenant in Christ saying, "Once you were not a people, but now you are God's people; Once you had not received mercy, but now you have received mercy."

God said to Moses, "You shall be for me a priestly kingdom and a holy nation."

Peter said, "You are a chosen race, a royal priesthood, a holy nation, God's own people, in order that you may proclaim the mighty acts of him who called you out of darkness into his marvelous light."

Moses told the people all the words of the LORD and all the ordinances; and all the people answered with one voice, and said, "All the words that the LORD has spoken, we will do."

Later, God said to the prophet Jeremiah: "The days are surely coming when I will make a new covenant with the house of Israel and the house of Judah. . . . . I will put my law within them, and I will write it on their hearts."

Moses built an altar at the foot of the mountain . . . . He sent young men of the people of Israel, who offered burnt offerings and sacrificed oxen . . . . Moses took half the blood and put it in basins, and half of the blood he dashed against the altar.

The Lord Jesus, on the night when he was betrayed, took bread . . . . He said, "This is my body that is broken for you."

Moses took the blood and dashed it on the people and said, "See the blood of the covenant that the LORD has made with you in accordance with all these words."

Jesus took a cup also, after supper, saying, "This cup is the new covenant in my blood. Do this as often as you drink it in remembrance of me. For as often as you eat this bread and drink this cup, you proclaim the Lord's death until he comes."

Thank you, gracious God, for the covenant you made with us through Moses.

Thank you, merciful God, for the new covenant you made with us through Christ.

Amen!

Amen!

Exodus 19:4-6; 24:3, 8
Jeremiah 31:31,33; 1 Peter 2:9-10; 1 Corinthians 11:23-26

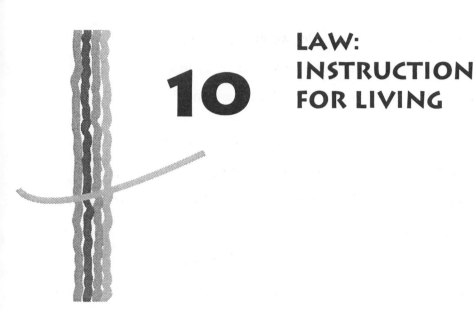

10 LAW: INSTRUCTION FOR LIVING

Background from the Author

Parts of Chapter 7 of *Theology in Exodus* will be relevant to this session. If you can obtain Walter Harrelson's book, *The Ten Commandments and Human Rights* (Philadelphia: Fortress Press, 1980), you will find it to be an excellent reference for your discussion of the Ten Commandments. My approach to the usefulness of Old Testament law for the Christian was developed in *Reclaiming the Old Testament for the Christian Pulpit* (Edinburgh: T. & T. Clark, 1980, reprint 1994, pp. 79-99).

People typically experience a certain "culture shock" when they read the Book of the Covenant with care, since this is not material the average Christian knows very well. The circumstances for which these laws were composed are so different from the way we live and the assumptions we make, that they take some getting used to. The fact that the code begins with regulations for slavery is no help, but you will see that the way slavery is treated throughout the Bible turns out to be a helpful clue as to the way we should understand law. Laws must change as people and societies change, or they will no longer be relevant. And, no law is perfect in itself; even the laws of the Bible are efforts to make the will of God work in a given human situation. The Old Testament contains the record of changes in law, as times changed, and that should not be a problem for us. Rather, it should be taken as the effort to come ever nearer to what God really wants of us. But there is something constant and unchanging, and that is God's intention. When we study the whole ethical teaching of the Bible, we can discover God's intention in the midst of the changes. Sometimes it is stated very clearly, as in Galatians 3:28; in other cases we can find it by tracing all that is said about a given ethical issue.

This is an important matter. For the most divisive issues in the churches today are not theological, but ethical; and Christians do not agree on the proper way to use scripture for guidance. Some quote a text, saying this is the eternal and unchangeable law of God. We see from the Old Testament that specific statutes did change, however. And we may be reminded that the Bible was used that way to defend slavery, although the Bible's whole message concerning slavery would not allow it. Others take the opposite position, saying it is all relative and changeable, and thus cannot be appealed to as authority for us. The subject requires a more lengthy treatise than this, but I hope this session will become the basis for useful discussions of the value of scripture for our decisions on what is the right thing to do.

One detail of the Book of the Covenant will certainly lead to questions: "You shall not boil a kid in its mother's milk" (Exodus 23:19b). Why not? The rabbis wondered about it, and concluded it must mean they should not eat meat products and milk products at the same meal. This mysterious statute thus became the basis for this aspect of the kosher food laws. That was probably not the original intent, however. It may have referred to a Canaanite cultic practice, and was thus forbidden because it would involve acknowledging other gods, but we cannot be sure of that. A recent theory points out that the mother's milk has a reddish tint for a few days after birth, and suggests it was thus associated with prohibiting the eating of blood. We cannot be sure of the reason at this point.

I have not dealt with 23:20-33 in this Session, since these verses allude to the journey to and occupation of Canaan, a quite different subject. The warning not to make covenants with the Canaanites will reappear in Chapter 34, and the angel will be referred to again in 33:2.

SESSION PLANS

Learning Objectives

This session is intended to enable participants to:

1. Cite several applications of the Ten Commandments to their lives and society.

2. Explain the purpose and evolution of legal codes such as the Book of the Covenant.

3. Describe the relationship between the law given in Exodus and the new covenant written on human hearts.

Resources You May Need

Bibles, chalkboard or newsprint and markers

Copies of Worksheet A, "The Ten Commandments" and Worksheet B, "Book of the Covenant"

Leadership Strategy

SETTING THE STAGE

1. **Prayer from the Psalms.** Read Psalm 119:33-40. If you want the group to read the Psalm together, photocopy it from "Prayers from the Psalms" in the Appendix. (3 minutes)

or

Opening Prayer. Open with a prayer thanking God for the life-giving gift of law for God's people. (3 minutes)

2. **Writing Laws that Define Identity.** Introduce today's theme as Law. Include the following information from page 92 in the *Resource Book*:

The Hebrew word *Torah,* which is usually translated "law," literally means "teaching." It is used of instruction of all kinds, and not just of rules for good conduct. This *teaching* defines our identity. It tells us who we are. The *Torah* defined what it meant to live as an Israelite. The ethical instructions of the New Testament define what it means to live as a Christian. These *teachings* describe the way the members of God's chosen people are to behave.

Divide into groups of 4-6. Have each group write some descriptive commandments for one of the following groups:

a. A fifth-grade class going on a field trip

b. A women's fellowship circle

c. A church softball team

d. A denominational office

e. A clergy retreat group

f. A confirmation class

Have representatives from each group read their commandments to the large group. As each group reads its "commandments," talk about how the commanded behavior reflects the identity of the group and relates to its purpose, goals, and situation. (15 minutes)

and/or

Review. Invite the group to recall highlights of last week's session on covenant by asking the following questions:

• What does it mean to be in Covenant with God?

• Who initiates this relationship?

• What does it mean to be holy?

Conclude the discussion by reminding the group of Dr. Gowan's words: "The first reason for obeying God is . . . gratitude." God initiates; we respond. The law outlines Israel's understanding of the response God wants. (10 minutes)

and/or

Naming Role Models. Read Psalm 1:1-3. Invite group members to think of people they have known whose lives are "like trees planted by streams of water" because they reflect the law of God in their lives. Have the participants talk together in pairs, with each naming the person that came to mind and describing how the rule of God was reflected in that person's life. (10 minutes)

EXPLORING THE SCRIPTURE

1. **Restating the Ten Commandments.** Give each person a copy of Worksheet A, "The Ten Commandments" and divide into four groups. Have each group discuss the meaning of the commandments assigned to them and then address the questions on the worksheet.

   After 15-20 minutes, bring the group together. Taking the commandments in numerical order, have a spokesperson from each group read the restated commandment and the grade it was assigned. (Note that there will be 2 reports for commandments 1 and 2.) (25-30 minutes)

   or

   Discussing the Commandments. Lead a discussion of the commandments as a whole. Ask:

   • What is the intent of the Ten Commandments?

   • What do the commandments reveal about the will of God?

   • How are they liberating?

- How are they being heard and not heard today? (You may want to focus this discussion on specific commandments.)

- Where and how does your church teach them? (10-15 minutes)

2. **Writing Covenants for Today.** Introduce the Book of the Covenant (Exodus 21:1-23:19), referring to Dr. Gowan's discussion of how codes evolve to meet needs for reform and to respond to new circumstances. Give each person a copy of Worksheet B, "Book of the Covenant." Then divide into 3 groups and make the following assignments:

Group 1 - Exodus 21

Group 2 - Exodus 22

Group 3 - Exodus 23

After about 15 minutes, reconvene the group and have a spokesperson from each small group read at least one of the reworded statutes to the large group. (20 minutes)

or

Comparing the Book of the Covenant with New Testament Passages. Ahead of time, print the following instructions on a newsprint sheet that will be visible to all, or on a separate sheet of paper or newsprint for each of 3 small groups:

Compare the following passages by answering these questions:

- How are the passages similar?

- How are they different?

- What is valuable about each type of law?

Divide into 3 groups and assign one pair of the following readings to each group:

Group 1: Luke 10:25-28   Exodus 21

Group 2:   Romans 12:9-21   Exodus 22

Group 3:   Romans 13:8-10   Exodus 23:1-19

After about 15 minutes, bring the group together, and have a representative from each group briefly summarize the group's conclusions. (20-25 minutes)

3. **Comparing Written and "Heart" Commandments.** Have volunteers read Jeremiah 31:31-34 and 2 Corinthians 3:1-4 aloud. Note the contrast between the Old Covenant written on stone and the New Covenant written by the Spirit on our hearts. Invite the group to think about the characteristics of written covenants and "Heart" or "Spirit" Covenants. List their observations in two columns on chalkboard or newsprint.

Written Covenants   *"Heart" or "Spirit" Covenants*

Then ask:

• What are the strengths and weaknesses of each kind of covenant?

• Is one to be preferred over the other? Why or why not?

• Are they incompatible? Why or why not? (10-15 minutes)

or

Discussion: Evolving Law. Refer to Dr. Gowan's discussion of the evolving attitude of the Bible and subsequent Christian teaching regarding slavery on pages 96-98 of the *Resource Book*. Note that lasting reform is often a gradual process. Have the group talk about why this is so. Invite them to think of present day laws, customs, and social institutions that some may think need to be reformed (e.g. health care system, education, physician-assisted suicide, gay and lesbian rights, etc.). Then have a volunteer read Romans 12:9-21. Ask:

• How does the ethic of this passage speak to the issues identified?

• What does this discussion teach us about the power of the law of love? (15 minutes)

CLOSING

1. **Sentence Prayers.** Invite group members to look over the Ten Commandments and pick one that has been meaningful for them today. Have them write a brief sentence prayer reflecting how it has spoken to them or asking for God's help in honoring it. Invite volunteers to read their prayers. After each prayer, the group may repeat the refrain: **"O Lord, our God, hear this prayer."** (8-10 minutes)

or

Litany and Prayer of Confession. Ask volunteers to read each of the 10 commandments, either from Exodus 20:1-17 or from the groups' restated commandments (Worksheet A). After each commandment is read, the group may respond with the following refrain: **"O God, write your commandment on my heart."**

Conclude with the following classic prayer or with a prayer of confession from your own denomination's liturgy.

> Most Merciful God, we confess that we have sinned against you in thought, word and deed, by what we have done, and by what we have left undone. We have not loved you with our whole heart: we have not loved our neighbors as ourselves. We are truly sorry and we humbly repent. For the sake of your Son Jesus Christ, have mercy upon us and forgive us; that we may delight in your will, and walk in your ways, to the glory of your name. Amen. (5 minutes) [*Book of Common Prayer, According to the Use of The Episcopal Church* (New York: Church Hymnal Corp., 1979), p. 352.]

or

Closing Prayer. Close with your own prayer giving thanks for God's gracious love and asking God to help us respond faithfully to his teaching. (3 minutes)

Looking Ahead

If you plan to take the Tour of the Tabernacle at the next session, designate a Tour Leader, Eleazer, and the Time Machine Conductor, photocopy a script for each of them, and finalize plans with them. If you plan to draw a diagram of the tabernacle, you may want to look for an illustration in a Bible dictionary.

The Ten Commandments

a. Restate the commandments to say what we shall do rather than what we shall not do.

b. Discuss how well your commandments are obeyed in today's society. Assign a letter grade (A, B, C, D, F) for each commandment to reflect the group's thinking.

Group 1

    1. You shall have no other gods before me.

    3. You shall not make wrongful use of the name of the Lord your God.

    7. You shall not commit adultery

Group 2

    2. You shall not make for yourself an idol

    4. Remember the Sabbath day, and keep it holy.

    8. You shall not steal.

Group 3

    1. You shall have no other gods before me.

    5. Honor your father and mother.

    9. You shall not bear false witness against your neighbor.

Group 4

    2. You shall not make for yourself an idol.

    6. You shall not murder.

   10. You shall not covet anything that belongs to your neighbor.

Worksheet B

Book of the Covenant

(Group 1—Exodus 21   Group 2—Exodus 22   Group 3—Exodus 23)

a. Select 3 statutes or verses that raise issues of social concern or justice (they may or may not seem relevant for today).
b. Discuss the general principle that may lie behind the particular code.
c. Then write a reworded statute for today's situation.

Selected Verses	Original Statute	Underlying Principle	Rewarded Statute for Today

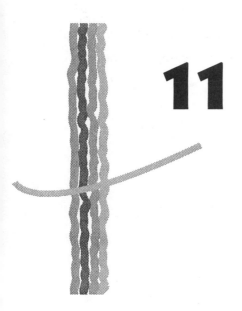

11

THE TABERNACLE: GOD CHOOSES TO DWELL AMONG HIS PEOPLE

Background from the Author

Chapter 3 in *Theology in Exodus* may be of some use to you as you prepare for this session. You or members of your group may find a little work by Brother Lawrence, *The Practice of the Presence of God*, to be of interest in connection with this subject. He was a monk in the 17th century who made it his aim to be conscious of God's presence with him at all times, and his comments on that way of life are well worth thinking about.

At one time the Church of England forbade preaching outside of a church building. John Wesley and his followers got into trouble for preaching in the open. Few of us would restrict worship in that way, and yet the church building has a special "aura" for many people. The subject of church buildings may be a sensitive subject in some places. As many congregations think about the forms of worship they are using, with differences appearing between the generations, it may be useful to begin the discussion of worship by asking what is needed for worship to occur. Beginning with what seems essential, you may move toward elements that are helpful. But along the way recall that in the materials from scripture we are using in this session, the essence of worship is coming into the presence of God.

The Babylonian Talmud, quoted at one point, is the full codification of Jewish law, completed around 500 A.D., and still used as the guide to the way Jews should live.

The tractate Megillah begins with rules for the reading of the Book of Esther at the festival of Purim, and then continues with discussions of synagogue worship in general.

SESSION PLANS

Learning Objectives

This session is intended to enable participants to:

1. List several of the most important features of the tabernacle.

2. State in their own words their understanding of the relationship between worship and place.

3. Describe how Christians have appropriated the temple tradition and theology.

4. Relate their own worship experiences to the Jewish tabernacle/temple traditions.

Resources You May Need

Bibles, chalkboard or newsprint and markers

Materials for the tabernacle tour including something to represent an altar (perhaps a table), something to represent a sacrificial animal (perhaps a stuffed toy), and a "bronze bowl" (any bowl will do) to hold the water that represents "blood of sacrifice"

3 copies of the "Tour of the Tabernacle" script

Copies of the worksheet "Where Does God Reside?"

Leadership Strategy

SETTING THE STAGE

1. **Prayer from the Psalms.** Read Psalm 139:1-12. If you want the group to read the Psalm together, photocopy it from "Prayers from the Psalms" in the Appendix. (3 minutes)

and/or

Opening Prayer. Offer your own prayer of thanksgiving for God's presence among the group. (3 minutes)

2. **Introducing the Tabernacle Theme.** Tell the group that because the tabernacle material in Exodus was probably written by priests, it contains many details that were more interesting to its authors than they are to us. Ask the participants to remember that amidst all the details, the central theme of this section is *coming into God's presence.* (2 minutes)

or

Relating the Tabernacle Material to Modern Church Planning. Introduce the discussion of the structure of the tabernacle by asking, "If our congregation were to build a new sanctuary, what special committees would we need? What experts might we employ?" List their answers on chalkboard or newsprint. Observe that many of the details involved in building a church would hold much more interest for specialized committees or experts than for the congregation in general. (For example, the congregation at large may not have strong opinions about what brand of dishwasher to buy or the number of circuit breakers required in an electrical panel.) Much of the description of the tabernacle in Exodus 25-31, 35-40 contains this very specific kind of information. The details were of particular interest to Israel's priests, who probably wrote this material. Their vocation was to preserve and protect the holiness of the sanctuary and to see that worship was properly conducted. While the details of the tabernacle are not important to us, thinking about the main points of this priestly material helps us understand more about Israel's worship and encourages us to think about our own worship. (8-10 minutes)

EXPLORING THE SCRIPTURE

1. **Tour of the Tabernacle.** Ahead of time, ask a volunteer to prepare to act as *Ithamar, son of Aaron*, and to lead "A Tour of the Tabernacle," using the script provided at the end of this session. Designate two other volunteers for the bit parts, *Eleazer* and *Time Machine Conductor.* The other members of the group

131

are to act as tourists who have traveled to the tabernacle in a Time Machine. Set up the "tabernacle," following the directions in the script, and take the tour. (20-25 minutes)

or

Diagram of the Tabernacle. Ahead of time, draw on newsprint or chalkboard a diagram of the tabernacle and court. The diagram should include three parts: (1) the most holy area containing the Ark of the Covenant, (2) the outer part of the tent containing the table for the "Bread of the Presence," the lampstand, and the altar for incense offering, and (3) the court. Base the diagram on an illustration provided in a Bible dictionary and on the following passages from Exodus:

- The most holy area: 25:10-22; 26:31-35; 37:1-9

- The outer part of the tent: 25:23-40; 30:1-10; 40:4-5, 22-27

- The court: 27:9-19; 38:9-20; 40:8

Invite discussion about the function of each part. Conclude the discussion by reminding the class that the purpose for the detailed provision for a holy place was to provide a place suitable for the Holy God to come near to the people. The tabernacle would be a place where God would meet with them and speak to them. (10-15 minutes)

2. **Small-Group Reports: Where Does God Reside?** Give each person a copy of the worksheet "Where Does God Reside?" Divide into six groups and assign each group one of the scripture passages on the worksheet. Each group is to discuss its assigned passage and work together to write a group statement.

    After about 15 minutes, reconvene the whole group and ask each small group to read its statement. Then, referring to pages 104-108 in the *Resource Book*, discuss the evolution of Israel's understanding of God's "place." Note that Jewish understanding of God's "residence" expanded to accommodate the destruction of the Temple in 70 A.D. Conclude with Dr. Gowan's statement, "Their conviction that God is universal, and by no means confined to the temple, led to the belief that when they gathered for worship in the synagogue, wherever it might be, God came to be present with them." (*Resource Book*, page 108) (25-30 minutes)

and/or

True Worship According to Jesus. Ask three volunteers to read John 4:7-24 as a dramatic reading, assigning each one a part: Narrator, Jesus, or the Samaritan Woman. You may want to create individual scripts by reproducing the passage and highlighting each part so that all will read from the same version. After the reading, title three columns on chalkboard or newsprint as follows:

When Jesus said,　　　　*she thought he meant,*　　　*but what he meant was*

Working together as a whole group, list Jesus' key statements and analyze their meaning by supplying the information required in the other two columns. Conclude the discussion by noting that Jesus taught that place is not important; Jesus' reference to worshiping in spirit and in truth affirms that God may be present to people anywhere through the Holy Spirit. (15 minutes)

3. **Earthly and Heavenly Tabernacles.** Dr. Gowan notes that the author of Hebrews made extensive use of the materials we have been studying concerning the tabernacle and priesthood as he developed an understanding of Jesus' death as a sacrifice (*Resource Book*, page 109). Ask each person to read one of the following passages from Hebrews. (Count off by threes or quickly divide the group into three sections, assigning each one a different passage.)

　　Hebrews 8:1-7

　　Hebrews 10:1-10

　　Hebrews 10:11-25

Give the participants a few minutes to read their assigned passages while you write the following headings on chalkboard or newsprint:

　　　　　　　　EARTHLY TABERNACLE　　　HEAVENLY TABERNACLE

Identity of priest

Place(s) of worship

Sacrificial offering

Effect of sacrifice

Working together as a whole group, supply information in both columns for each topic. Then ask, "What does the author of Hebrews want readers to know about the role of Jesus? What difference does this suggest between Christianity and Judaism?" Refer to the section "The Heavenly Temple, and Hope for a New Jerusalem" for help in guiding this discussion. (10-15 minutes)

and/or

A New Heaven and a New Earth. Just as the Jewish people had to refine their understanding of God's place during the exile and after the destruction of the Temple, the persecution of the early Christians gave rise to new ways of understanding the older traditions and images. Invite the group members to listen quietly as two volunteers read aloud Revelation 21:1-4 and 22:1-5. Ask, "What emotions and thoughts do these passages evoke? What longings or needs lie behind human endeavors to find God's 'place of residence'? How does understanding the tabernacle and temple traditions help us gain new insights about our own understanding of God's 'place of residence'?" Refer to the section "The Heavenly Temple, and Hope for a New Jerusalem" in the *Resource Book* for help in guiding this discussion. (10-15 minutes)

3. **Thinking about Our Own Worship.** In groups of 3-6, talk about the participants' own experience of worship. Introduce the discussion in words similar to these:

> By building the tabernacle, the people of Israel created a hallowed space for worship. Think about our own place of worship and the rituals of our service. What helps you feel God's presence? What changes could help you feel closer to God in worship? What is the value of having designated worship spaces? What are limitations and risks of placing strong emphasis on a particular worship space?

After 15-20 minutes, bring the groups together and ask a volunteer from each group to summarize the most important points of their discussion. (30-35 minutes)

or

Personal Reflections. Invite participants to reflect on their own sense of God's presence. On chalkboard or newsprint, draw this continuum:

TODAY, I FEEL GOD AS

CLOSE TO ME
OR WITHIN ME--DISTANT

    1   2   3   4   5   6   7   8   9   10

Observe that in the tabernacle, God came down from the mountain to dwell among the people. Ask, "Right now, today, do you experience God more as distant (up on a mountain) or intimate (close or within you)? Where would you place yourself on this continuum? Give yourself a score from 1 to 10, with 10 being 'most distant' and 1 being 'within me.' " Then invite the participants to talk with a partner about why they placed themselves where they did and how they feel about being in that place. (10 minutes)

CLOSING

A Prayer. Close with the following prayer:

> O God, in the tabernacle you dwelt in the midst of our faith ancestors, saying these words: "I will be their God. And they shall know that I am the Lord their God, who brought them out of the land of Egypt that I might dwell among them." Later, Jesus reminded us that we ourselves are a tabernacle, a dwelling place for your Spirit. Open our hearts to your Spirit within us, Gracious God, that we may worship you in spirit and in truth. Amen. (3 minutes)

and/or

Your Own Prayer. Offer your own prayer thanking God for allowing each person to be a dwelling place for the Spirit and asking for increased openness to God's presence. (3 minutes)

Looking Ahead

The next session suggests portraying contemporary idols by making posters or collages. For this activity you will need light posterboard or large construction paper. If you use the collage option, you will also need a stack of old magazines. Another exercise asks the group to look through hymns to find images of God as *changing* or *unchanging*. For this activity you will need a hymnal for each person, including if possible, several different hymnals. It will be helpful for you to pre-select several hymns to get the group started. Some possibilities are "Immortal, Invisible, God Only Wise," "God Moves in a Mysterious Way," "There's a Wideness in God's Mercy," and "Great Is Thy Faithfulness." You will find other examples as you look through some of your congregation's favorite hymns.

A Tour of the Tabernacle

Participants: (1) *Ithamar*, the youngest son of Aaron, who conducts the whole tour, (2) *Eleazer*, who enters, pantomimes the ritual cleansing of hands and feet in preparation for entering the tabernacle, and exits without speaking, and (3) *the conductor of the Time Machine*, who calls "All aboard" from offstage. All the others in the group are tourists visiting the tabernacle.

Setup: The entire "tour" takes place in the court of the tabernacle. Designate a space to function as this court. If a vacant room is available, the whole room could be the "court" with a door at one end serving as the "court gate" and a door at the other end serving as the entrance to the tabernacle itself (which the group is not allowed to enter). A hallway or the church narthex is another possibility. If a separate room is not available, you might designate space within your learning area, marking the entrance to the court and the tabernacle by setting two chairs placed back-to-back but separated to form "gates." Also designate something to represent the following:

> *altar of sacrifice* (about halfway between court entrance and tabernacle entrance. This might be a small table or two chairs, seats together.)

> *bronze bowl for ritual cleansing* (between altar of sacrifice and tabernacle entrance. This could be any large bowl from the church kitchen placed on a table or chair. Use lots of imagination. No elaborate props are needed.)

Ithamar: Welcome, visitors from the 21st century! I hope your trip in the Time Machine was smooth. I am the priest Ithamar, the youngest son of Aaron, Moses' brother. I understand that you would like to see our tabernacle. My father has agreed to grant you the privilege of taking a tour. I am pleased to be your escort. Your tour guide has given me a copy of your Bible. Such an amazing book! I understand you have been reading the Book of Exodus, so you know that my people, the people of Israel, constructed this portable dwelling place for Yahweh our God in the wilderness near Mount Sinai.

You may enter the court here, through the gate. (*Pulls back imaginary curtains, guides "tourists" through the "entrance."*) Notice that the gate is a screen made of blue, purple, and crimson yarn. (*Pauses for all to enter the "court."*)

You are now in the court that surrounds the tabernacle. Notice how large it is! It is 100 cubits long and 50 cubits wide. That's 150' x 75' in your way of measuring. The walls of the court are white curtains made of fine twisted linen. Aren't they lovely? The curtains separate the tabernacle and its court from the Israelites' camp which is all around it. The tent that you see ahead is the tabernacle. The court goes all around the tabernacle.

(*Moves to the altar and turns to face the group.*) Come forward now to the altar. Stand in front of it, please. Notice that it is a hollow box made of acacia wood and bronze. This is the place where we make animal sacrifices to Yahweh. We priests eat some of the sacrificial meat.

In the Bible your tour guide gave me, I read that King Solomon will eventually build a temple for Yahweh. It will be modeled after this very tabernacle and court. It won't be portable. But it will have an altar like this one for animal sacrifice. Your tour guide showed me the Gospel story about Jesus' cleansing the temple. That will happen in the temple court, which will be patterned after this court where you are standing.

(*Moves to the bowl.*) Walk around the altar now and come forward to this bronze bowl. This is where we priests wash our hands and feet for ritual cleansing before we enter the tabernacle.

(*Moves and stands in front of tabernacle entrance.*) Come forward again, where you can get a good view of the entrance to the tabernacle. Don't come too close, though; it's a holy place. Notice that the tabernacle's sides are curtains made of violet, purple, and scarlet fabric. Cherubim are woven into the fabric. Cherubim are guardian spirits from the heavenly realm. They have the body of a lion, the wings of an eagle, and a human face. Aren't the curtains exquisite! Now look up. See? The tent that covers the tabernacle is made of goats' hair and rams' skins.

Are any of you Jewish priests? No? Then I can't allow you to come any farther. I'm sorry. Only priests are allowed to enter the tabernacle itself. If you were allowed to walk through

138

this screen and go into the tabernacle, you would enter its outer part. That is a holy place, but not the *most* holy place. On one side of the holy place is a table where the bread of the presence is kept. The bread of the presence is our symbolic offering to Yahweh, and we replace it with fresh bread every week. On the other side is a golden candlestick with seven candelabra. And in the center, in front of the entrance to the most holy place, is an altar where we offer perpetual incense to Yahweh. We priests replenish the incense every morning and every evening. (*Looks to horizon.*) I see the sun is getting low now, so it's just about time. Ah, yes. Here comes my brother Eleazer now. Let's clear a path so he can purify himself before he enters the tabernacle to tend the incense. (*Eleazer enters, pantomimes the ritual washing of hands and feet in the bowl, and exits into the "tabernacle." While the ritual cleansing is taking place, Ithamar continues.*) Notice Eleazer is wearing a robe over a long tunic. He's also wearing an ephod—that's a linen apron that priests wear, and a turban. Everything he is wearing has been handmade from the finest materials. (*Waits for Eleazer to exit.*)

The tabernacle has two parts. The outer part, which I've just described, is separated from the inner part by a veil that is made of material of many colors and embroidered with cherubim. Beyond this veil is the most holy place; that's where the Ark of the Covenant is. Inside the ark are the tablets of the law. At the top of the ark is a slab of pure gold, called the mercy seat. A gold cherub sits at each end.

I wish you could see the ark and the cherubim, but I can't permit it. Even I can't enter the most holy place! The only time I get to see the Ark of the Covenant is when we take the tabernacle down to move it. Only the high priest is allowed to move beyond the veil to enter the most holy place, and he only enters it once a year. I was very surprised to read in your Gospels of Matthew and Mark that this veil will be torn in two from top to bottom on the day when your Jesus dies on the cross. I find that very hard to understand. It sounds like just about anybody would have access to God.

(*Speaks quietly, with awe.*) See the cloud over the most holy place? That means Yahweh is present right now! The ark is Yahweh's dwelling place. That's what *tabernacle* means, you know—dwelling place.

Wherever we go, we take our tabernacle with us. The whole structure is completely portable. So no matter where we are, the holy God dwells in our midst. We just hope we can be a people holy enough so that Yahweh will be able to continue to live among us.

(*Voice of the Time Machine conductor calls from a distance,* **"All aboard!"**) It sounds like your Time Machine is starting its countdown. You'd better be on your way. Thank you for visiting our tabernacle. May Yahweh dwell with you also.

Where Does God Reside?

A subcommittee of the Roman Senate is conducting a survey throughout the empire. Your group has been asked to issue a statement answering the question, "Where does God reside?" You are to base your statement on one of the following passages:

Group 1: Exodus 19:9-22

Group 2: Exodus 29:42-46

Group 3: 1 Kings 8:22-30

Group 4: Jeremiah 7:1-15

Group 5: Ezekiel 11:14-25

Group 6: John 4:7-24

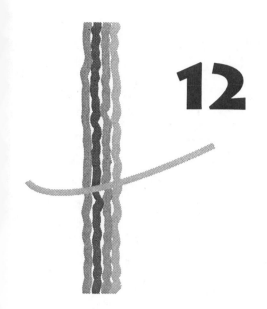

12 THE GOLDEN CALF: ISRAEL'S "FALL STORY"

Background from the Author

Two good resources that help us better understand the meaning of idolatry in our own time are Harrelson's book, *The Ten Commandments and Human Rights*, pp. 61-72, and J. B. Phillips' book, *Your God Is Too Small* (New York: Macmillan, 1964). Parts of Chapter 8 of *Theology in Exodus* should be helpful, also.

The Jewish sources mentioned in the second paragraph are midrashes. These are rabbinic commentaries on the books of the Bible, probably dating from the seventh to ninth centuries A.D.

There are problems of continuity in Chapters 32-33. In Chapter 32, the episode involving the Levites doesn't seem to fit, as I note briefly in the *Resource Book*. In Chapter 33, a description of the tent of meeting interrupts the dialogue between Moses and God (33:7-11). Some scholars have tried to sort things out and find a better order, but without success. It looks as though we may have here a collection of memories of incidents in the wilderness, without exact recall as to when each of them occurred. At any rate, if we don't get too frustrated by trying to make a clear, continued story of it, each paragraph is meaningful in itself. I have sometimes thought that since sin, in itself, is an absurdity, a neat, clear discussion of it would not correspond to reality. And the whole burden of Chapter 32-34 is sin, and what God does about it.

The violence of the Levite incident remains a problem for us, however. Neither priests (descendents of Aaron) nor Levites look very admirable in Chapter 32. We know that there was rivalry at times over who was qualified to serve as priests, and that leads us to wonder whether those who disapproved of the descendents of Aaron managed to have their point of view reflected in this story. One thing is clear. When the kingdom was divided after the death of Solomon, Jeroboam I, who ruled the Northern Kingdom, established sanctuaries at Dan and Bethel as rivals of Jerusalem. He set up golden calves there, and the author of 1 Kings 12:26-30 obviously associates the action with the sin of the golden calf at Sinai.

In the early period Levites (members of the tribe of Levi) served as priests. See Judges 17:7-13. In the post-exilic period they were not allowed to serve at the altar or in the temple, but carried out other duties: singers, guards, etc. As a tribe, in the very early period they seem to have had a reputation for ferocity, as in Exodus 32 and Genesis 49:5-7. Note that there are two different opinions of their violent behavior in these two texts. In the *Resource Book* I just point out that the violence in Chapter 32 accomplishes nothing, and I think that is more important than the puzzling reference to ordaining themselves for the service of the LORD.

That the Old Testament says God occasionally has a change of mind will be a surprise to some readers. I devoted a fair amount of space to it because it proves not to be a problem but an important insight. It says God really does respond to us, that what we do really makes a difference with God. It seems at first to be a problem because traditional Christian theology has emphasized that God is unchangeable, immovable. That also implies unfeeling, but this is more the God of Greek philosophy, which strongly influenced the development of Christian theology, than of scripture. The fact that the texts show God changing away from judgment, in favor of mercy, also makes God's changeability great news. It is an important insight into God's own character.

Note the ways the NRSV tries to smooth over the apparent contradiction in 1 Samuel 15:11, 29, 35, by translating the same Hebrew verb in three different ways. God did have a change of mind about Saul, the chapter says twice, so what of verse 29? Samuel's statement must then be taken as a reference to that particular divine decision—God will not restore Saul to favor, and will not waver regarding that decision—and not as a general statement about how God acts in every case.

Forgiveness is introduced in this session, but will be the main subject of Session 13, so extended discussion of that should be reserved for the next time.

SESSION PLANS

Learning Objectives

This session is intended to enable participants to:

1. Relate Israel's worship of the golden calf to the sin of idolatry in their own lives.

2. Contrast Moses' and Aaron's responses to the people's sin.

3. Cite some examples of God's nature as both changing and unchanging.

Resources You May Need

Bibles, chalkboard or newsprint and markers

3 x 5 cards or slips of paper, posterboard or construction paper, markers, old magazines

Copies of a prayer of confession used in your congregation's worship

Copies of Worksheet A, "Personal Time Chart" and Worksheet B, "The Nature of God in our Hymns"

Leadership Strategy

SETTING THE STAGE

1. **Prayer from the Psalms.** Read Psalm 51:1-4. If the group is to read the Psalm together, photocopy it from "Prayers from the Psalms" in the Appendix. (3 minutes)

and/or

Opening Prayer. Open with a prayer inviting God to be part of today's reflection and learning. (3 minutes)

2. **Introducing the Theme.** Introduce today's subject as the story of the golden calf. Invite the group to review Exodus 24:12-18 and 32:1-6 and to "set the scene" together. Ask:

   • Where are the Hebrews at this point in the Book of Exodus?

   • Where is Moses as Chapter 32 begins?

   • What are the people doing while Moses is on the mountain? (5 minutes)

or

Reading the Scripture as Drama. Read aloud Exodus 32:1-24, assigning parts for Aaron, The People, The LORD, Moses, Joshua and a narrator. (To involve more people, you might assign a different narrator for each paragraph.) Use Bibles of the same translation, or make a copy of one translation for each reader. (5 minutes)

and

Making Excuses. Invite group members to imagine that they are among the Hebrew people who helped make the golden calf. Now imagine Moses returning and seeing what they have done. He exclaims, "How could you have done this?" As the participants spontaneously call out excuses list them on chalkboard or newsprint. (10 minutes)

EXPLORING THE SCRIPTURE

1. **Examining Personal Idols.** Read Matthew 22:37 and Acts 17:22-31. Then quote this statement from the *Resource Book*: "Belief in the one God requires a radical decision: Nothing—repeat, nothing comes before God." Distribute copies of Worksheet A, "How I Spend My Time" to each person. After allowing time for group members to complete the worksheet, invite them to talk about their observations and feelings about this exercise in groups of three. (20-25 minutes)

and/or

Picturing Contemporary Idols. Remind the group of the people's words: "These are your gods, O Israel, who brought you up out of the land of Egypt." In groups of 3-4, brainstorm what a visitor from space would surmise to be our gods based on our TV shows, commercials, and movies. Have each group make a poster depicting one of these gods. (Another option is to give each group a variety of magazines with which to create a collage for their chosen "god.") After 15-20 minutes, bring the group back together to report on the cultural gods they have identified. (20-25 minutes)

and/or

Discussion: "Sacred" Idols. Consider together the possibility that even sacred things can become idols, that is, replacements for God. Ask, "What are examples of sacred things that can become idols?" (Examples might include a Bible text, the law, a creed, a tradition, a building.) "What happens when such things become replacements for God?" (10 minutes.)

and/or

Writing a Definition of Sin. Discuss together what the group sees as major problems in our time. What connections do they see between these problems and the sin of idolatry? Based upon this discussion and the material in Chapter 32, invite each person to write a definition of sin. Invite those who are willing to do so to read their definitions. (15 minutes)

2. **Preparing "Fitness Reports" for Moses and Aaron.** The Navy holds the captain of a ship responsible for everything that happens. Invite participants to skim Exodus 32 and prepare "Officer Fitness Reports" on Moses and Aaron. List the following "Fitness Categories" on chalkboard or newsprint, and have the group rate Moses and Aaron on each category as "Excellent, Fair, or Poor," citing examples.

Following orders of superiors

Relationship with subordinates

Taking responsibility

Personal integrity

Then ask, "What other categories might be included in the report? How does Moses' response to the people's sin contrast with Aaron's blaming behavior? What happens when leaders blame their followers?" (10-15 minutes)

or

Discussion: Moses as Intercessor. Ask, "In Exodus 32, what are some ways Moses tried to deal with the people's sin?" List their answers on chalkboard or newsprint. The list may include pleading with God (11-13), destroying the idol (19-20), accusing Aaron (21), punishing the guilty (25-29), and trying to atone (30-33). Then ask, "What approach(es) seemed most effective? What was God's reaction to Moses' pleas for the people? What does this suggest about our own intercessory prayer?" (10 minutes)

3. **Bible Research: God's Nature as Changing/Unchanging.** Ahead of time, print each of the following Bible references on separate 3 x 5 cards or slips of paper. Give one to each participant. You need not use all the scripture references.

Genesis 6:6,7	Judges 2:18	1 Samuel 15:11,29,35
2 Samuel 24:16	Jeremiah 4:28	Jeremiah 18:8,10
Jeremiah 20:16	Jeremiah 42:10	Jeremiah 26:3,13,19
Ezekiel 24:14	Joel 2:13,14	Amos 7:3,6
Jonah 3:9,10	Jonah 4:2	Zechariah 8:14
Psalm 90:13	Psalm 106:45	Psalm 110:4

Have each group member read his or her passage aloud. As each is read ask, "What does this passage imply about God and about God's relationship to humankind?" Some group members may point out the apparent contradiction in 1 Samuel 15 between verse 29 which says that God does not change, and verses 11 and 35, where God's mind is changed about Saul. Note Dr. Gowan's explanation in "Background from the Author" that Samuel's statement in verse 29 must be taken as a reference to a particular divine decision—God will not restore Saul to favor—and not as a general statement about how God acts in every case. After all the references are read ask, "Do you find it helpful or troublesome to think of God as changing?" List their thoughts on chalkboard or newsprint, using these categories:

Helpful   *Troublesome*

Then read this statement from the *Resource Book*:

Rather than seeing this [God's changing] as a problem, we can find . . . insight into the nature of God. It is what makes forgiveness and intercessory prayer possible. It means God really does respond to what people do and ask.

After eliciting responses to this idea, conclude with Dr. Gowan's interpretation: "What is unchangeable is God's intention to save." (15-20 minutes)

or

Research: God's Nature in Hymns. Many well-known hymns present images of God that emphasize different aspects of God's nature. Distribute Worksheet B, "The Nature of God," and a hymnal to each person. Use several different hymnals. Invite group members to look through the hymnal and write phrases from the hymns in the appropriate quadrant of the worksheet. List a few hymns on chalkboard or newsprint, including:

Immortal, Invisible, God Only Wise

God Moves in a Mysterious Way

There's a Wideness in God's Mercy

Great is Thy Faithfulness

After about 10 minutes, make a composite list on chalkboard or newsprint. Invite people to share the images or phrases they most resonate with. Then ask, "Can all of these images be valid ways to picture God?" Finally, recall that Dr. Gowan states God's "changing" in response to what people do and ask is what makes forgiveness possible and ask, "What is your reaction to that statement?" (15-20 minutes)

CLOSING

1. **Prayer of Confession.** Read a prayer of confession and words of assurance that are used in your congregation's worship. If these are not printed in your hymnal or prayer book, ask your minister for an appropriate prayer. (3 minutes)

and/or

Silent Prayers of Confession. Invite the group to think silently about the story of the golden calf and to think about ways they too fail to love God with their whole heart. Allow time for silent confession; then offer a prayer of thanksgiving for God's mercy.

and/or

A Hymn. Say or sing "Great is Thy Faithfulness." (3 minutes)

Looking Ahead

As the end of the Exodus study draws near, you may want to begin planning a special celebration for the last session, perhaps special refreshments or a potluck lunch or dinner. You may also want to announce plans for a future study.

Personal Time Chart

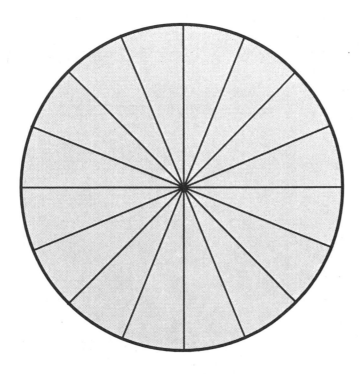

Based upon a "typical" 16-hour waking day, select one or more pie pieces to represent the ways you spend your time. Use various shadings or colors to create a legend for identifying the various sections.

1. How do you think God is or is not part of each activity?

2. Do any of these activities seem closer to worshiping "shrines made by human hands" than worshiping "the God who made the world and everything in it?" (Acts 17:24)

3. How could each piece of your pie reflect the words of Acts 17:28: "In God we live and move and have our being"?

The Nature of God in Our Hymns

UNCHANGING   RESPONSIVE (CHANGING)

JUDGING   MERCIFUL

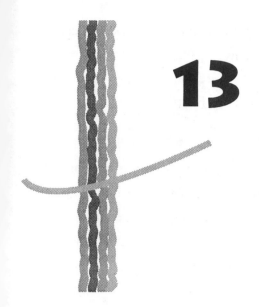

13 FORGIVENESS: FOUNDATION FOR THE FUTURE

Background from the Author

Moses' strange reactions to God in Chapter 33, which I have described as appearing as though he did not hear, may be a problem of continuity—paragraphs that originally did not go together as they are now. I have offered a different reading, however, taking them to be perhaps an accurate reflection of great uncertainty about whether an apparently insoluble problem—human disobedience—can be dealt with successfully.

My comments about the use of the word "face" in Hebrew to mean "presence" are intended to encourage participants not to take the puzzling references to God's back literally. There is more on this in note 21, page 286 of *Theology in Exodus*, which may or may not be helpful. In the *Resource Book* I emphasize that the point of the passage is that there is nothing that can be seen that reveals God. Note that after God says he will do this (33:21-23) nothing more is said about it, except that God passed before Moses (34:6). What is important is what God says.

You may want to do your own word studies of the key terms in Exodus 34:6-7 in preparation for this session. Pages 236-238 of my book may be helpful. Note especially what I have said about mercy, and you may want to think about the cross in connection with that. It may also help with the familiar problem we have with human forgiveness. How can we be forgiving without seeming to condone sin?

It would seem appropriate at this point to encourage some forgiveness. It is not an easy subject to discuss. The past cannot be undone, but the issue in forgiveness is whether one can be freed from the past as shackles that dictate what the future must be. The message of scripture is that God does not want to hold our past against us, but desires to free us for a better future. It is not easy for everyone to believe.

An example: a pastoral counselor told me of a woman with whom he was just beginning to work. He soon discovered that the bitter feelings she had against her mother kept coming up in every discussion, and he told her, "You will not be able to make any more progress toward health until you can forgive your mother for what she has done to you." The resentment she carried was part of what was making her sick. This is a case that didn't necessarily call for repentance on the mother's part. We don't know whether forgiveness would have changed the mother at all, or whether it would have helped the relationship, but the counselor was convinced it would help the patient.

A different example: In 1981 a man tried to assassinate Pope John Paul II. Later the Pope learned that in prison the man began to regret what he had done and expressed his repentance. When the Pope visited the man who had tried to kill him, and forgave him, that created some debate. Forgiveness is not well-understood, or accepted. The man was forgiven by the one he had tried to kill, but he stayed in prison. What had changed? If it was real forgiveness, there would have been changes within both men. The Pope would hold no ill feelings toward his would-be killer and would desire only good for him. The man would no longer brood over what he had done, but would be able to put that behind him and think about what good he could make of the rest of his life. You may have better examples to offer.

SESSION PLANS

Learning Objectives

This session is intended to enable participants to:

1. Describe the dilemma that human sin created for God.

2. Compare God's mercy and forgiveness in Exodus 33-34 with the concept of grace in John 1:1-18.

3. Define forgiveness.

4. Tell or write about their own need for forgiveness.

Resources You May Need

Chalkboard or newsprint and markers

Bibles

3 x 5 cards

Copies of the worksheet "Forgiveness and Forgiven-ness," and the litany "The Word Tabernacled Among Us"

Leadership Strategy

SETTING THE STAGE

1. Justice-Mercy Continuum. Ahead of time, draw this continuum on chalkboard or a wide sheet of newsprint. (You may tape two sheets of newsprint together, end to end, to make a wider sheet.)

I see God as a God of

JUSTICE--MERCY

As people arrive, ask them to place an "x" (no names) on the line representing the place where they see themselves on the continuum. Post this continuum or mark off its section of the chalkboard, so it will remain visible throughout the whole session. (5 minutes)

2. Prayer from the Psalms. Read aloud Psalm 51:9-12. If you want the group to read the Psalm together, photocopy it from "Prayers from the Psalms" in the Appendix. (3 minutes)

and/or

Opening Prayer. Offer your own prayer asking for God's mercy. (3 minutes)

3. **Review.** Review briefly the situation of the people of Israel at the close of last week's session by asking the group to recall the details or by summarizing it in words similar to these:

> At the close of last week's session, we saw the people, led by Aaron, making a golden calf and worshiping it. Before Moses even got down from the mountain with the tablets, the people had broken the first two commandments! God threatened to destroy all the people of Israel except Moses, but Moses persuaded God to reconsider. Still, God had a great dilemma. (5 minutes)

EXPLORING THE SCRIPTURE

1. **Listing Arguments: God's Decree and Moses' Plea.** Title two sheets of newsprint or two columns on a chalkboard "I WON'T GO WITH YOU" and "PLEASE COME!" Read aloud Exodus 33:1-5. Ask, "Why won't Yahweh go with the people?" Write their answers under the "I won't go" column. The answers should bring out the idea that distance between God and the people is necessary because the holy God cannot co-exist with sin.

Read aloud Moses' plea in Exodus 33:15-16. Ask, "What arguments does Moses give as he pleads with God to reconsider?" Write their answers under the "Please come!" column. The answers should indicate that God's presence makes Israel distinct from other people and shows that God is pleased with Moses. They may also include points brought out in the last session: God should not break the promise made to Israel or waste the effort already invested in this people. (10 minutes)

or

Role Playing: Moses and God. Read aloud Exodus 33:1-5 and 33:15-16. Ask all the group members to pair up with a partner other than a spouse. Then divide the room in half, with an equal number of pairs on both sides. Add a third person to one or two groups if necessary in order to have the same number of groups on both sides. Instruct half of the pairs to talk with their partners about what Moses might say to try to persuade God to come with the people. Instruct the other half to discuss how God might explain to Moses reasons for the decision not to come. After about five minutes, direct each of the "Moses pairs" to move to the other side of the room and join up with a "God pair." The newly-formed foursomes are to talk together; the "Moses pair" and the "God pair" each try to persuade the other to their point of view. After about 5 minutes, conclude the exercise by stating that for a God of justice, human sin poses a great dilemma because the holy God cannot coexist with human sin. The distancing, which the people lament and Moses tries to change, is actually for their protection. (20 minutes)

2. **Discussion: God's Mercy.** Referring to the "Justice-Mercy" continuum, lead a discussion about God's mercy and forgiveness. Point to the "Justice" end of the continuum, and convey in your own words the following information:

> Relationship with God, broken by the golden calf incident, cannot be restored by an appeal to God's justice. Nor can it be restored by human effort because people will continue to sin. Although human beings long for close relationship with God, we don't—and can't—deserve it. The answer to the dilemma—the only possible answer—is found in a revelation about the character of God. God is *merciful and forgiving*. (Point to the "Mercy" end of the continuum.)

Then ask a volunteer to read aloud Exodus 34:6-7. (5 minutes)

and

Comparing Exodus 33-34 and John 1:1-18. The section "Grace and Truth: John's Use of Exodus 33-34" in the *Resource Book* demonstrates that the Prologue to the Gospel of John (John 1:1-18) contains many echoes from Exodus 33-34. These echoes are particularly clear in John 14:16-18. Read aloud the following lines, one at a time. After reading each line, ask, "What words or ideas in Exodus 33-34 seem to be reflected in this line?" Note the responses on the chalkboard or newsprint. Add any points from Dr. Gowan's discussion that the group fails to bring out.

And the Word became flesh and lived (tabernacled) among us

and we have seen his glory,

the glory as of a father's only son, full of grace and truth.

From his fullness we have all received, grace upon grace.

The law indeed was given through Moses;

grace and truth came through Jesus Christ.

No one has ever seen God.

It is God the only Son, who is close to the Father's heart, who has made him known.

After the group has identified Exodus echoes for each of these lines, read aloud Dr. Gowan's summary in the last two paragraphs of Session 13, beginning about the middle of the second-to-last paragraph, with "No one has ever seen God . . . " Then ask:

- How is John's use of *grace* similar to the concept of God's mercy and forgiveness in Exodus 33-34?

- How is the coming of Christ a fulfillment of what had been promised at Sinai? (15 minutes)

3. **Defining Forgiveness.** Ask, "How would you define *forgiveness*?" Guide the discussion to bring out the main points in the section "Merciful and Gracious" in the *Resource Book*.

- Forgiveness does not remove the consequences of our actions.

- Sin always produces suffering, for the sinner and for others.

- Forgiveness means that the relationship with God that had been broken by sin can be reestablished because God will not hold it against the repentant sinner.

- Past sins, repented and forgiven, need not dictate what the future must be. (5 minutes)

Completing Sentences about Forgiveness. Title two sides of a chalkboard or two sheets of newsprint, "Forgiveness IS . . . " and "Forgiveness is NOT . . . " Ask the participants to finish each of these sentences in as many ways as they can, calling out words or phrases as they occur to them. Write their suggestions in the appropriate column. After the group has listed a variety of conclusions to both sentences, have two volunteers read aloud Exodus 34:6-7 and Psalm 103. Ask, "How does the knowledge that God forgives us help us to forgive others?" (10 minutes)

4. **Reflection and Sharing: Forgiveness and Forgiven-ness.** In groups of 4-6, complete the worksheet, "Forgiveness and Forgiven-ness." Explain that the worksheet calls for a period of quiet reflection before any discussion takes place. Announce the length of this quiet period (10-15 minutes), and suggest that each group designate a timekeeper. Remind the group that they are to choose only *one* of the questions to share with the group. Emphasize that they are to tell the group only what they feel comfortable talking about. Urge the groups to listen without comment to each person and to divide their time so that all group members have the opportunity to talk. (35-40 minutes)

or

Reflection and Writing: Need for Forgiveness. Ask the group to think quietly about this question:

In my life right now, how do I need to be forgiven by a particular person and/or by God?

After 4-5 minutes of quiet, give all the group members a 3 x 5 card. Ask them to write on the card a sentence or two that expresses the words of acceptance or forgiveness they would most like to hear spoken by another person or by God. Tell them you will read the cards aloud, without names, as part of the closing prayer; therefore they should phrase their sentences in words they are willing for the group to hear. Also note that any who wish to retain their cards may do so. When they have finished writing, collect the cards of all who are willing to contribute them. (15 minutes)

CLOSING

1. **A Litany.** Read responsively the litany, "The Word Tabernacled Among Us." Introduce the litany by saying,

    > The prologue to the Gospel of John makes many references to the part of Exodus we studied today. In the *Resource Book*, Dr. Gowan states: "These texts from Exodus seem to bring us nearer to God than any other part of the Old Testament, and it appears that John recognized that. As he developed this magnificent hymn in praise of the Incarnation, God coming to dwell with us as a human being like us, he found that what had been promised at Sinai had come true in Jesus."

    As you designate who will read each part, mention that the parts printed in plain type quote Exodus; the parts printed in bold quote John. (5 minutes)

    and/or

    Words of Forgiveness. Close with the following prayer, based on Psalm 103. If the group has written words of forgiveness they hope to hear on cards, incorporate their sentences into the prayer.

    > O Lord, you are merciful and gracious, slow to anger and abounding in steadfast love. You do not deal with us according to our sins, nor do you repay us according to our iniquities. Trusting your mercy, we confess our sin. We have hurt others and ourselves and you. We long to be forgiven. We wait to hear words of acceptance and forgiveness from parents, siblings, children, friends, and others, but their lips are silent. Please, O God, let us hear those words from *you*, spoken out of your steadfast love.

    > *(Read slowly each card from the exercise, skipping over any that are repetitions. If the group did not do this activity, pause for silent reflection.)*

    > As the heavens are high above the earth, so great is your steadfast love toward those who fear you. As far as the east is from the west, so far you remove our transgressions from us. Bless the Lord, O my soul. All that is within me, bless your holy name. Amen. (8-10 minutes)

2. **Closing Prayer.** Offer your own prayer of thanksgiving to the God who is merciful and gracious, slow to anger, and abounding in steadfast love and faithfulness. (3 minutes)

Looking Ahead

The final session suggests presenting "Moses: This Is Your Life." If you decide to use this option, ask a volunteer to play the part of Moses. So that "Moses" can come prepared to ad lib responses to the characters who will appear, give the volunteer the list of characters and scripture references outlined in this activity.

The session also asks participants to reflect on the whole Exodus study, using the worksheet, "Thinking Back on our Study." You may want to distribute this worksheet (located in the resources for Session 14) at the close of this session so that group members can think about it as they prepare for the final session.

Finalize any plans you are making for a special celebration at the closing session. The "celebration" might include a potluck lunch or dinner or special refreshments. Also announce any plans your congregation has for another study.

Forgiveness and Forgiven-ness

*Think quietly about the following sets of questions. Then choose **one** of these sets and talk about your answer to that set with your group.*

1. When have you felt forgiven by another person and/or by God?

   How did this forgiven-ness feel?

   How did it change your attitudes, actions, or relationships?

2. Whom do you need to forgive?

   Why is this forgiveness difficult for you to grant?

3. How do you need God's forgiveness in your life right now?

Which of the following statements comes closest to the way you feel about God's forgiveness?

Why?

- God won't or can't forgive this particular wrong because_____.

- God will forgive me if _____.

- God has already forgiven me.

Litany: "The Word Tabernacled Among Us"

Yahweh said to the people of Israel: "I will dwell among you, and I will be your God." (Exodus 29:45)

The Word became flesh and tabernacled among us. (John 1:14)

Moses asked Yahweh, "Show me your glory." (Exodus 33:18)

The Word became flesh and tabernacled among us, and we have seen his glory, the glory as of a father's only son. (John 1:14)

When Yahweh passed before him, Moses heard these words: "Yahweh, Yahweh, a God merciful and gracious, slow to anger and abounding in steadfast love and truth." (Exodus 34:6)

The Word became flesh, . . . full of grace and truth. From his fullness we have all received, grace upon grace. (John 1:14, 16)

The law was given through Moses. (Exodus 20)

The law was indeed given through Moses; grace and truth came through Jesus Christ. (John 1:17)

Moses asked Yahweh, "Show me your ways." Yahweh told Moses, "I will make all my goodness pass before you, and will proclaim before you the name, 'Yahweh'." But you cannot see my face; for no one shall see me and live. (Exodus 33:13, 19-20)

No one has ever seen God. It is God the only Son, who is close to the Father's heart, who has made him known. (John 1:18)

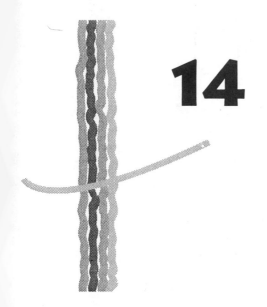

14

EXODUS AS A BASIS FOR THEOLOGICAL REFLECTION

Background from the Author

My suggestions for this final session are to be found in the *Resource Book*, so there is little to add here. As you prepare, if you follow the same route of review and reflection that I suggest for every participant you should be ready to lead an effective concluding discussion. My own reflections tended to focus on what we learn about God from this approach, and you will understand the reasons for that. I think the suggestion that Burrows' full list of topics be used as a basis for review should leave the way open for everyone's interests to be pursued.

SESSION PLANS

Learning Objectives

This session is intended to enable participants to:

1. Recall the main characters and events of Exodus.

2. Describe some of the insights they have gained from the study.

3. Compare theological insights they have gained from Exodus with Millar Burrows' list of major theological themes.

4. Talk about ways this study has spoken to them personally.

Resources You May Need

Bibles

Chalkboard or newsprint and markers, typing paper

A table or altar, a cross for the altar if desired

3 x 5 cards

Copies of Worksheet A, "Response to the Murmurers," Worksheet B, "Important Theological Themes," and Worksheet C, "Thinking Back on our Study"

Leadership Strategy

SETTING THE STAGE

1. **Prayer from the Psalms. Read Psalm 99.** If you want the group to read the Psalm together, photocopy it from "Prayers from the Psalms" in the Appendix. (3 minutes)

and/or

Opening Prayer. Pray in your own words, thanking God for the past weeks of learning and fellowship and asking God's blessing on the group as the study draws to a close. (3 minutes)

2. **Presenting "This Is Your Life."** Ask someone to play the role of Moses while members of the group act as key figures in the Exodus story, presenting Moses' life story in the manner of the TV program, "This Is Your Life." (It will be helpful to designate "Moses" ahead of time and to give him or her the list of characters who will participate so that "Moses" can ad-lib appropriate responses.) Divide into groups of 2-3. Give each group a 3 x 5 card on which you have printed one of the names listed below. Smaller groups need not use

all the names. Tell the groups that they will have 5 minutes to write in 30 words or less what they will say to Moses when they appear on "This Is Your Life."

Shiphrah or Puah, the midwives (Chapter 1)

Moses' mother (Chapter 2)

Miriam (Chapters 2, 15)

Daughter of Pharaoh (Chapter 2)

Pharaoh (Chapters 2-14)

Zipporah, Moses' wife (Chapter 2)

Jethro (also called Reuel), Moses' father-in-law (Chapter 3, 18)

Aaron (Chapters 4, 24, 32). (15 minutes)

or

Naming the Characters. Invite the group to see how many characters they can name from the Book of Exodus in 5 minutes. List the characters on chalkboard or newsprint as they are called out, and invite the group to say a few words about what each one did. (5 minutes)

EXPLORING THE SCRIPTURE

1. **Responding to Negative Comments.** Distribute Worksheet A, "Response to the Murmurers." Divide into groups of 3-6 and assign each group a name, Carl, Gloria, or Don. Ask them to write a response to the comment made by their assigned person. (If the group is large, you may need to assign the same name to more than one group.) After about 15 minutes, bring the whole group together and have spokespersons from each group read their letters. (20-25 minutes)

or

Creating an Exodus Commercial. In groups of 5-6, develop a 1-minute commercial promoting a study of the Book of Exodus. Present the commercials to the large group. (20 minutes)

Listing Insights. Invite participants to look at the Table of Contents of the *Resource Book* and call out insights they have gained from the study of Exodus. List their insights on chalkboard or newsprint. (10 minutes)

2. **Theological Themes in Exodus.** The *Resource Book* listed 15 major theological themes, organized in a very traditional way. This list is taken from *An Outline of Biblical Theology* by Millar Burrows. Comparing this list with insights participants have gained from Exodus may be a helpful way to review and summarize the Exodus study. Give each person a copy of the worksheet "Important Theological Themes." Divide into groups of 3-6 and assign two, three, or four of the themes to each group, depending on the time available. Invite the groups to discuss what they have learned from Exodus on each assigned topic. Point out that Exodus does not deal with every one of the theological categories. If they do not recall an insight from Exodus on a particular theme, they should simply note that. After about 20 minutes, reconvene the group and have a spokesperson from each group briefly summarize the group's findings. Then ask, "What insights that you gained from the study of Exodus seem most important to you personally?" (40 minutes)

or

Sharing insights, questions, and priorities. Distribute a copy of Worksheet B, "Important Theological Themes" to each participant. Using the information in the section "Exodus as a Basis for Theological Reflection" in the *Resource Book*, introduce the list of theological themes indicating its source and briefly explaining the meaning of each category. Print the following instructions on chalkboard or newsprint. Then invite the participants, working individually, to review the list and to respond as indicated:

- Put a *star* (*) in front of the 3 areas which you believe are most important for Christian discipleship.

- Put a *question mark* (?) in front of those areas (no more than 3) about which you have deep questions or doubts.

- Put a *minus* (-) in front of those areas (no more than 3) which have a low priority for you.

- Put a *plus* (+) in front of those areas (no more than 3) that you would like to explore further.

After 5-10 minutes, invite the participants to share their responses for each category, working in groups of three. Encourage them to explain their reasons for the markings they made. After about 20 minutes, reconvene the whole group. Ask, "What new insights into the nature of God or our relationship with God have you gained from this study of Exodus?" (40 minutes)

3. **Sharing Personal Reflections.** Divide into groups of 3-6. Write the following questions on chalkboard or newsprint that is visible to all, or write these questions ahead of time on a separate sheet of newsprint or typing paper for each small group.

- What is the most important thing for your own life that you have learned in this study?

- What has been the most difficult subject or idea you have encountered?

- What have you found in this study that you think the church most needs to hear?

Note that these are the "Questions for Reflection" in the *Resource Book*. Suggest that the group invite each person to answer the first question before going on to the second, allowing each person to speak without interruption and being careful to divide time equally. Tell them that they will have 20-30 minutes for this small-group sharing.

Bring the whole group together, and ask them to call out things they have learned and things they think the church needs to hear. List these on chalkboard or newsprint. (30-40 minutes)

Thinking Back on our Study. Distribute Worksheet C, "Thinking Back on our Study." Allow 8-10 minutes for participants to complete the worksheet. Then invite them to talk about their answers with a partner. Groups of 10 or fewer may wish to do this reporting as a whole group. If you plan to use "Sharing Memories" as part of the closing, postpone reporting on item 4 on the worksheet, "an insight, memory, or feeling I will take away from this study," until the closing. (20-25 minutes)

4. **Refreshments.** If you have planned special refreshments or a meal for this session, this may be the best time to serve it. You may also want to announce plans for a future study. (20-45 minutes)

CLOSING

1. **A closing ritual.** Choose one of the options below. Give the following instructions for that option and allow time for the group members to prepare their offerings. All participants do the same option.

   a. Pick a favorite passage (not more than 3 verses) from the book of Exodus.

   b. Go outdoors if weather permits, and find and bring back something that reminds you of something meaningful from the Exodus study. For example, a rock might remind you of the tablets of the commandments. A flower might remind you of God's blessing. A branch might be a reminder of the burning bush.

   c. Remembering that Moses heard the voice of God in the burning bush, think about what you have "heard" (or felt) as the voice of the Spirit during this time together. Write one thing you have "heard" on a 3 x 5 card.

   After finishing a, b, or c above, invite all the participants to join in a closing circle. If you chose option **b**, prepare a table or altar for their selections. You may wish to put a cross on this altar.

   Begin this time together with your own personal sharing. Then invite participants to share their offerings, one by one, reading their favorite verse or words they "heard," or placing their object on a designated "altar" as they describe briefly what it symbolizes to them. After each person's offering, sing or say a verse of the hymn "Blest Be the Tie That Binds." (15-25 minutes)

or

Sharing Memories. Allow a few minutes for quiet reflection on the items below. (If the group has not done Worksheet B, "Looking Back on our Study," allow a little extra time for reflection.) Then form a circle and invite participants, in turn, to describe both of the following:

- something that surprised me

- something I will take away from this study (10 -20 minutes)

2. **Closing Prayers.** Suggest that members of the group may want to offer their own prayers as the study comes to a close. Tell them that you will open the time of prayer and that all who wish to do so may offer their own prayers. Begin with your own prayer of thanksgiving for this time together, naming any specifics you feel are important. Then invite the participants to offer their own prayers by saying, "Hear now the prayers that we offer." (5-8 minutes)

and/or

Benediction. Close the study by reading the words God spoke to Moses in Exodus 19:4-6:

> You have seen how I bore you on eagles' wings and brought you to myself. Now therefore, if you will obey my voice and keep my covenant, you shall be my own possession among all peoples. You shall be to me a kingdom of priests and a holy nation. (1 minute)

Response to the Murmurers

Suppose your friend Carl, Gloria, or Don makes one of the following comments:

Carl says: **"Why study the Old Testament? What do those old stories have to do with me?"**

Gloria says: **"I don't like the OT! It's all about law and judgment! I want to get to the New Testament so we can talk about grace and mercy."**

Don says: **"Maybe there's a God out there somewhere, but it doesn't sound to me like that God is very involved with what's going on around here."**

Write a letter responding to the person assigned to your group.

Dear (Carl, Gloria, or Don) . . . ,

Important Theological Themes

The *Resource Book* included the following list of 15 major theological themes, taken from Millar Burrows' book, *An Outline of Biblical Theology*:

GOD

CHRIST

THE UNIVERSE

MAN

THE PEOPLE OF GOD

THE DIVINE REQUIREMENT

SIN

JUDGMENT AND SALVATION

ESCHATOLOGY (STUDY OF LAST THINGS) AND THE FUTURE LIFE

THE WAY OF SALVATION

THE CHRISTIAN LIFE

SPECIAL OFFICES AND FUNCTIONS

PUBLIC WORSHIP

CHRISTIAN SERVICE

MORAL AND SOCIAL IDEALS

Thinking Back on Our Study

Think about the following questions, and jot down a few notes about how you wish to answer each one.

1. An "Aha!" for me was

2. A question I have is

3. An Exodus story that felt like *my* story is

4. An insight, memory, or feeling I will take away from this study is

Appendix

Prayers from the Psalms

(Note: additional devotional aids can be found in the Kerygma
publication *Meeting God in the Bible* by Donald L. Griggs
which is available from the Kerygma office.)

Psalm 61:1-3 (for Session 2)

Hear my cry, O God; listen to my prayer.

From the end of the earth I call to you, when my heart is faint.

Lead me to the rock that is higher than I;

for you are my refuge, a strong tower against the enemy.

Psalm 9:1-2, 9-10 (for Session 3)

I will give thanks to the LORD with my whole heart;

I will tell of all your wonderful deeds.

I will be glad and exult in you;

I will sing praise to your name, O Most High.

The LORD is a stronghold for the oppressed,

a stronghold in times of trouble.

And those who know your name put their trust in you,

for you, O LORD, have not forsaken those who seek you.

Psalm 67:1-2 (for Session 4)

May God be gracious to us and bless us

and make [your] face to shine upon us,

that your way may be known upon earth,

your saving power among all nations.

Psalm 46:8-11 (for Session 5)

Come, behold the works of the LORD;

 see what desolations he has brought on the earth.

He makes wars cease to the end of the earth;

 he breaks the bow, and shatters the spear; he burns the shields with fire.

"Be still and know that I am God!

 I am exalted among the nations, I am exalted in the earth."

The LORD of hosts is with us;

 the God of Jacob is our refuge.

Psalm 66:1-12 (for Session 6)

Make a joyful noise to God, all the earth;

 sing the glory of his name; give to him glorious praise.

Say to God, "How awesome are your deeds!

 Because of your great power, your enemies cringe before you . . . "

Come and see what God has done: he is awesome in his deeds among mortals.

 He turned the sea into dry land; they passed through the river on foot . . .

Bless our God, O peoples,...

 For you, O God, have tested us; you have tried us as silver is tried . . .

you let people ride over our heads; we went through fire and through water;

 yet you have brought us out to a spacious place.

Psalm 114 (for Session 7)

When Israel went out from Egypt, the house of Jacob from a people of strange language,

 Judah became God's sanctuary, Israel his dominion.

The sea looked and fled; Jordan turned back.

 The mountains skipped like rams, the hills like lambs.

Why is it, O sea, that you flee? O Jordan, that you turn back?

 O mountains, that you skip like rams? O hills, like lambs?

Tremble, O earth, at the presence of the LORD, at the presence of the God of Jacob,

    who turns the rock into a pool of water, the flint into a spring of water.

Psalm 23 (for Session 8)

The LORD is my shepherd, I shall not want.

    He makes me lie down in green pastures;

he leads me beside still waters;

    he restores my soul. . . .

Even though I walk through the darkest valley, I fear no evil;

    for you are with me; your rod and your staff—they comfort me.

You prepare a table before me in the presence of my enemies;

    you anoint my head with oil; my cup overflows.

Surely goodness and mercy shall follow me all the days of my life,

    and I shall dwell in the house of the LORD my whole life long.

Psalm 105:1-8 (for Session 9)

O give thanks to the LORD, call on his name,

    make known his deeds among the peoples…

Seek the LORD and his strength;

    seek his presence continually.

Remember the wonderful works he has done,

    his miracles, and the judgments he uttered,

O offspring of his servant Abraham,

    children of Jacob, his chosen ones.

Psalm 119:33-40 (for Session 10)

Teach me, O LORD, the way of your statutes, and I will observe it to the end.

    Give me understanding, that I may keep your law and observe it with my whole heart.

Lead me in the path of your commandments, for I delight in it.

    Turn my heart to your decrees, and not to selfish gain.

Turn my eyes from looking at vanities; give me life in your ways.

   Confirm to your servant your promise, which is for those who fear you.

Turn away the disgrace that I dread, for your ordinances are good.

   See, I have longed for your precepts; in your righteousness give me life.

Psalm 139:1-12 (for Session 11)

O LORD, you have searched me and known me.

   You know when I sit down and when I rise up; you discern my thoughts
      when I am far away.

You search out my path and my lying down, and are acquainted with all my ways.

   Even before a word is on my tongue, O LORD, you know it completely.

You hem me in, behind and before, and lay your hand upon me.

   Such knowledge is too wonderful for me; it is so high that I cannot attain it.

Where can I go from your Spirit? Or where can I flee from your presence?

   If I ascend to heaven, you are there; if I make my bed in Sheol, you are there.

If I take the wings of the morning and settle at the farthest limits of the sea,

   even there your hand shall lead me, and your right hand shall hold me fast.

If I say, "Surely the darkness shall cover me, and the light around me become night,"

   even the darkness is not dark to you; . . . for darkness is as light to you.

Psalm 51:1-4 (for Session 12)

Have mercy on me, O God, according to your steadfast love;

   according to your abundant mercy blot out my transgressions.

Wash me thoroughly from my iniquity,

   and cleanse me from my sin.

For I know my transgressions, and my sin is ever before me.

   Against you, you alone, have I sinned, and done what is evil in your sight,

so that you are justified in your sentence

   and blameless when you pass judgment.

Psalm 51:9-12 (for Session 13)

Hide your face from my sins,

> and blot out all my iniquities.

Create in me a clean heart, O God,

> and put a new and right spirit within me.

Do not cast me away from your presence,

> and do not take your holy spirit from me.

Restore to me the joy of your salvation,

> and sustain in me a willing spirit.

Psalm 99 (for Session 14)

The LORD is king; let the peoples tremble!

> He sits enthroned upon the cherubim; let the earth quake! . . .

Moses and Aaron were among his priests, ...

> They cried to the LORD, and he answered them.

He spoke to them in the pillar of cloud;

> they kept his decrees, and the statutes that he gave them.

O LORD our God, you answered them;

> you were a forgiving God to them, but an avenger of their wrongdoings.

Extol the LORD our God, and worship at his holy mountain;

> for the LORD our God is holy.